A STUDENT'S COMPANION FOR

The Bedford Guide for College Writers

A STUDENT'S COMPANION FOR
The Bedford Guide for College Writers

Elizabeth Catanese
Community College of Philadelphia

Copyright © 2023 by Bedford/St. Martin's.

All rights reserved. No part of this book may be reproduced, stored in a retrieval system, or transmitted in any form or by any means, electronic, mechanical, photocopying, recording, or otherwise, except as may be permitted by law or expressly permitted in writing by the Publisher.

For information, write: Bedford/St. Martin's, 75 Arlington Street, Boston, MA 02116

ISBN 978-1-319-48550-4

INTRODUCTION

A Student's Companion for The Bedford Guide for College Writers reinforces the most foundational elements in academic writing. While recognizing and respecting your abilities, this supplement breaks down the steps necessary to excel in college writing, build confidence, tackle time management, and write ethically; it provides additional activities to help you draft, revise, and edit college-level work; and it provides sentence guides for academic writing, as well as editing practice. This companion, meant to supplement the coverage in *The Bedford Guide for College Writers*, gives you additional support for your composition class. For your instructor, it is an ideal solution for accelerated learning programs or co-requisite courses, while the deep integration with *The Bedford Guide for College Writers* makes it an ideal resource for any instructor who wants students to build a strong foundation in academic writing.

Part One: Succeeding in College

Part One addresses topics that are critical to your success: confidence building, time management, and ethical and responsible writing. This coverage can be a handy reference outside of class.

Part Two: Writing Activities

Part Two of this workbook will help you break down writing tasks for each of the key chapters in *The Bedford Guide for College Writers*:

- Recalling and Observing
- Interviewing for Information
- Comparing and Contrasting
- Explaining Causes and Effects
- Taking a Stand
- Proposing a Solution
- Evaluating and Reviewing
- Supporting a Position with Sources
- Responding to Literature
- Responding to Visual Representations

To successfully complete any writing assignment, you must break down the assignment into a series of steps. Whether these steps are explicitly mapped out or intuitively known, a paper cannot materialize out of thin air. This workbook simplifies writing tasks into manageable steps, with additional useful activities. These activities will help you with the technical aspects of writing, as well as the potential cognitive or emotional hang-ups that can get in the way of the writing process. For example, you are asked to brainstorm, but you are also asked to identify what assignments are asking you to do and to write down what, for you personally, might get in the way of starting an assignment.

In my career as an assistant professor of English at Community College of Philadelphia, I have found that most questions during office hours are along the lines of "How do I start?" or "What exact steps do I follow?" This workbook is, in a sense, office hours in workbook format. For some questions, there is truly no single "right" response, which is why there is no answer key. However, every activity will generate material for you to ponder and discuss.

Part Three: Additional Tools for Practice

Part Three begins with sentence guides that help you learn to present information and ideas to others, present your own views, and then put the pieces together to write an effective academic essay. If you need additional help, you can also get practice with editing sentences and paragraphs, reviewing the parts of speech, writing correct sentences, managing punctuation, mechanics, and spelling, and more. You can choose the areas where you need to grow, or your instructor can point you to activities based on the specific struggles that emerge in your papers.

The overall goal for this workbook is to help you become an increasingly engaged, professional, and happy writer. Have a wonderful semester!

Elizabeth Catanese
Assistant Professor, English
Community College of Philadelphia

CONTENTS

Introduction   v

PART ONE: Succeeding in College   1

1 Building Your Confidence   3

Not Feeling Confident   3

Identifying Strengths and Setting Goals   4
    The Confidence Checklist   4

Learning from Your Experiences and Choices   5

Taking Risks   6
    Taking Risks in the Classroom   6
    Speaking Up in Class   6
    Exercise: Questions and Answers   7

Examining Emotions   7
    Exercise: What Makes a Success?   7

Being Persistent   7
    Assertiveness Check-Up   8

Being Assertive   8

Developing a Network   9

Advice from Other Students   9
    The Goal Setter: Liberal Arts Major at the Community College of Rhode Island   9
    The Networker: Marketing Major at Bryant University, Rhode Island   10
    Tips for Confidence-Building   10

2 Managing Your Time   11

The Case for Time Management   11

Taking Charge of Your Time   12
    Setting Goals   12
    Knowing Your Priorities   13

Control Factor: Know What You *Can* and *Can't* Control   14
    What You *Can* Control   14
    What You *Can't* Control   14

Four Time-Wasting Habits to Avoid   15
    1. Procrastinating   15
    2. Overextending Yourself   15
    3. Losing Your Focus   16
    4. Running Late   16

Two Indispensable Tools to Keep You on Track   16
    A Planner or Calendar   16
    A To-Do List   17

Advice from Other Students   18
    Easy Ways to Maximize Your Time   18

3 Writing Ethically and Responsibly   20

Defining "Cheating"   20

The Cheating Problem   21

Why You Shouldn't Cheat   21

Why It's Easy to Get Caught   22

How *Not* to Cheat: Ten Essential Tips   22
    The Penalties for Cheating   22

The Rules of Paraphrasing   24

PART TWO: Writing Activities   25

4 Recalling and Observing   27

Pre-assignment Questions   27

Understanding Your Assignment   28

How to Write an Observation   28

How to Write from Recollection   30

5 Interviewing for Information   32

Pre-assignment Questions   32

Understanding Your Assignment   33

How to Write an Essay Based on an Interview   33

6 Comparing and Contrasting 36

Pre-assignment Questions 36

Understanding Your Assignment 37

How to Write a Compare and Contrast Essay 37

7 Explaining Causes and Effects 42

Pre-assignment Questions 42

Understanding Your Assignment 43

How to Write a Cause-and-Effect Essay 43

8 Taking a Stand 46

Pre-assignment Questions 46

Understanding Your Assignment 47

How to Write an Argumentative Essay 47

How to Write a Counterargument 49

9 Proposing a Solution 51

Pre-assignment Questions 51

Understanding Your Assignment 52

How to Write a Proposal 52

10 Evaluating and Reviewing 54

Pre-assignment Questions 54

Understanding Your Assignment 55

How to Write an Evaluation 55

11 Supporting a Position with Sources 57

Pre-assignment Questions 57

Understanding Your Assignment 58

How to Write an Essay that Supports a Position with Sources 58

12 Responding to Literature   61

Pre-assignment Questions   61

Understanding Your Assignment   62

How to Write about Literature   62

13 Responding to Visual Representations   65

Pre-assignment Questions   65

Understanding Your Assignment   66

How to Write about Visual Representation   66

PART THREE: Additional Tools for Practice   69

14 Sentence Guides for Academic Writers   71

Academic Writers Present Information and Others' Views   72
    Presenting What Is Known or Assumed   72
    Presenting Others' Views   73
    Presenting Direct Quotations   73
    Presenting Alternative Views   74

Academic Writers Present Their Own Views   74
    Presenting Your Own Views: Agreement and Extension   74
    Presenting Your Own Views: Queries and Skepticism   75
    Presenting Your Own Views: Disagreement or Correction   75
    Presenting and Countering Objections to Your Argument   76

Academic Writers Persuade by Putting It All Together   77
    Presenting Stakeholders   77
    Presenting the "So What"   77
    Presenting the Players and Positions in a Debate   78
    Using Appropriate Signal Verbs   78

15 Writing Grammatically Correct Sentences   80

Correcting Sentence Boundary Issues   80
    Identifying Subjects and Verbs   82
    The Implied You   82
    Correcting Sentence Fragments   83
    Your Sentences   83
    Run-Ons and Fragments in Context   83
    Run-Ons and Fragments in the Real World   83
    Pronouns   84
    Pronouns in Your Work   85

16 Writing Clear Sentences in a Thoughtful Style 86

Sentence Combination 86

Sentence Combination in Your Work 88

Subject/Verb Agreement 88

Conjugations 88

Vocabulary Development in Papers 90

Specificity and Precision of Language 91

Description and Paragraph Expansion 92

Transitions 94

Research Skills 95
    Paraphrasing 95
    Paraphrasing Steps 96
    Quotation Sandwich 96
    Paragraph Incorporating Quotation 97

17 Activities for Improving Your Writing 98

Revision Activity 98

Peer Review Activity 98

Thesis Statement Activity 99

Topic Sentences Activity 99

Using Models Activity 100

A STUDENT'S COMPANION FOR

The Bedford Guide for College Writers

PART ONE

Succeeding in College

1. Building Your Confidence   3
2. Managing Your Time   11
3. Writing Ethically and Responsibly   20

Building Your Confidence

Confidence can help drive and shape your experiences as a student, performer, athlete, employee, parent, and the many other roles you play in your life. True confidence is often defined as having a positive and realistic belief about yourself and your talents and traits. *Assertive, optimistic, eager, proud, independent, trustworthy,* and *mature* are some of the many terms associated with someone who has true confidence. Conversely, a lack of confidence can result in a poor performance in those same roles.

Here are just a few reasons to develop confidence:

- **Confidence helps sell who you are.** Knowledge, skills, and experience are necessary and important. If you do not possess and project an air of confidence, others may not realize you have these qualities.
- **Confidence reassures others.** It can create trust in the people in your life, whether they are your peers, classmates, coworkers, or loved ones.

This guide explores the role that confidence plays in everyday success and offers strategies on building your confidence levels around all of the roles you play in your life.

Not Feeling Confident

Have you had any trouble maintaining your confidence since you started college? It may surprise you to learn that you are not the only first-year student who feels this way. Many students who enter college for the first time feel just like you do: not very certain of all that lies ahead and unsure how to deal with a number of challenges, both in and out of the classroom. Below are just a few steps you can take to help develop more confidence:

- **Take a strengths inventory.** Make a list of what you're good at.
- **Set measurable, attainable goals.** Ask yourself what you want to accomplish in the next week, month, or year, and then break those goals up into smaller, short-term goals.

- **Take responsibility for your actions.** Make a consistent effort to learn from your experiences (the good and the bad) and own your choices.
- **Dare to take intellectual risks.** Question assumptions, and ask yourself if the things you believe to be true actually are.
- **Examine and acknowledge feelings.** When something bothers you, ask why.
- **Take charge and be persistent.** Remember, luck is 99 percent perseverance.
- **Assert yourself.** When you want something, you've got to ask.
- **Remember, you're not alone.** Identify individuals who exhibit confidence, and make a strong effort to model the types of behavior that make the greatest impression on you.
- **Believe in yourself.**

Identifying Strengths and Setting Goals

Why not start building your confidence by reminding yourself what you are good at? You can start with this simple, yet effective, activity:

Make a list of what you believe are your strongest skills and qualities. Take the time to think deeply and honestly about this exercise before you start. Another way to do this is to ask yourself: "When I feel like I am at my best, what am I doing?" Continue performing those activities to create an increased sense of confidence.

Long-term goals vs. short-term goals: How do they differ? A crucial part of developing, building, and maintaining your confidence is to set long- and short-term goals that you can reach and that are able to meet your expectations. Think of long-term goals as the final product and short-term goals as the steps along the way. For example, if you were to write a ten-chapter novel, you'd have ten short-term goals (write a chapter) and one long-term goal (write a novel).

THE CONFIDENCE CHECKLIST

Before examining a series of meaningful steps you can take to build confidence, let's start with the following confidence checklist. How would you respond to the following statements? Be as completely truthful and objective as you can be.

	Yes	No
I believe I know what is best for me.	☐	☐
I feel I am a genuine person.	☐	☐
I am extremely tolerant of others in my life.	☐	☐
I am consistent — I do as I say.	☐	☐
I avoid procrastinating.	☐	☐

	Yes	No
I take an active role in classroom discussions.	☐	☐
I have an inner voice that guides my decisions.	☐	☐
I maintain good eye contact and tone of voice when speaking.	☐	☐
I often doubt myself.	☐	☐
I am able to handle constructive criticism.	☐	☐
I have difficulty trusting others.	☐	☐
I prefer being alone than being with groups of people.	☐	☐
I would describe myself as an outgoing and assertive individual.	☐	☐
I feel I am capable of assessing my true capabilities.	☐	☐
I am an optimistic person by nature.	☐	☐

If you answered "no" to more than half of the statements, your level of confidence is likely not where you want it to be — and you're probably not alone! Keep reading for some proven strategies to boost your confidence.

Now it's your turn.

- Select one goal you would like to achieve in the next month. Be specific about what that goal is.
- Now identify two or three effective actions you will take to obtain this goal. Once again, be specific and include a time frame for performing these actions.
- Think of one possible barrier that might prevent you from reaching this goal.
- Now consider one action you will take to overcome this barrier. Be sure to detail what this action will be.
- Last, predict what you honestly believe will be your degree of success in eventually achieving this goal.

> **TIP**
>
> So how does setting goals help build confidence? Think about it this way: If you set up a series of short-term goals you know you can achieve, aren't you going to feel more confident each time you check off one of those goals? Even better, aren't you going to feel like a rock star by the time you achieve your ultimate long-term goal? There is nothing that builds more confidence than seeing hard work pay off.

Learning from Your Experiences and Choices

Wisdom can often be gained through both good and bad experiences and through the outcomes of the choices we make. If you can accept that you are ultimately the one responsible — not others — for your actions, this is the first important step to practicing this philosophy while in college.

One strategy for maintaining this belief is to not play the blame game; for example, if you received a low grade, be honest with yourself and ask what role you played in earning the grade. Admitting you are the one responsible for your actions and then responding (and learning) from that outcome will help strengthen your self-esteem and confidence.

Taking Risks

Has anyone ever said, "Nothing ventured, nothing gained" to you? To take a risk can be an unsettling challenge — you can't be sure it will be worth it, you may question whether you have the ability and the desire to attempt something, and you might think about the consequences of that risk if you are unsuccessful.

Now that's the negative approach. What if you turned this around and, instead, took a chance on something daunting? What if you decided that no matter what obstacles got in your way or what doubts crept into your mind, you would continue to pursue whatever you set out to accomplish? Imagine how you will feel when the results turn out to be positive ones.

Another way of thinking about this is "If you remain in your comfort zone you will not go any further." While taking a risk can seem difficult at first, it almost always pays off in the end — especially in the classroom.

Taking Risks in the Classroom

Your instructors have probably urged you to question rather than to simply accept everything you read or hear. If you follow this advice, you'll take risks in the classroom all the time — intellectual risks, otherwise known as critical thinking. You do this when you speak up in class, when you write an essay, and whenever you carefully rethink long-held beliefs.

Speaking Up in Class

The reward for intellectual risk taking is that you come away with a better understanding of yourself and the world around you. But what if you are terrified of speaking up in class and of saying something dumb? What if you simply don't know where to start? Below are two case studies to help you start thinking about how to better approach intellectual risks.

Student A read the class material twice and completed all the assignments. She came to class prepared to take notes and was ready and willing to listen to what the instructor had to say on the topic being presented. As an adult student, she was used to participating in meetings at work, and she didn't feel nervous about speaking up, so she didn't think that she needed to prepare any additional material.

Student B also completed the assigned homework and believed he knew the material but also knew he would be reluctant to share his thoughts or respond to questions posed to the class. As a strategy, he wrote down several questions and responses to what he assumed would be a part of the class discussion. When he attended class, he referred to his questions and answers when those areas of discussion came up.

What were some strategies that each student employed that would help them take intellectual risks? Who do you think came to class better prepared? For each case study, what would you recommend the student do differently next time?

Exercise: Questions and Answers

What do you do to prepare for class discussions? Both Student A and Student B are good students. They read the material and did their assignments. Student B, however, uses higher-level thinking questions to help stimulate critical thinking. As you prepare for class, try to use the following generic question stems to ask questions about the material covered. Then take a few minutes to jot down your answers.

What would happen if _____?
What is the difference between _____ and _____?
What are the implications of _____?
Why is _____ important?
What is another way to look at _____?

Examining Emotions

Daniel Goleman, author and creator of the theory of emotional intelligence (EQ), stresses the vital role EQ plays in building self-confidence. One of his key components is Emotional Self-Management, or the ability to make sensible decisions even when your emotions tell you to do otherwise. For example, if you received a failing grade on a quiz, your first impulse might be to get angry. Even worse, you might consider dropping the class. A better strategy would be to take the time to examine why you earned the grade that you did and to allow yourself the time needed to learn how to succeed in the course. Examining your feelings and how you react to certain situations can keep you from giving up too early on something that is challenging.

Exercise: What Makes a Success?

Make a list of the qualities you see in people you think of as confident. Share the list with someone else in your class and discuss which of these qualities have to do with feelings and interactions with other people. How many of these qualities do you see in yourself?

Being Persistent

One of the simplest ways to gain confidence is to be persistent. *Persistence* simply means the ability to stick with something through completion, even if you don't always want to. If a task or challenge seems difficult at times and the outcome may be uncertain, persistence helps you keep at it. Let's look at an example:

Imagine that you are frustrated with the teaching style of one of your instructors. She presents the material in a way that doesn't work for you (but it seems to do so for your classmates). You can elect to drop the class early in the semester and perhaps have a different teacher next time, or you could take steps that will allow you to persist in the course, such as working with a tutor, forming a study group, or meeting with your professor for clarification. In the end, you will not have given up, and your outcome could likely be a favorable one.

Ultimately, it is *your* responsibility to take charge of your success and persist — even if you have some setbacks at first. When you feel like you may be about to give up, remind yourself of your long-term goals and how persisting at the current task will help you attain those goals.

ASSERTIVENESS CHECK-UP

Answer the following questions as honestly as you can:
- Do you express your point of view even when it is not the same as others'?
- Will you actually say "no" to a request made by friends or coworkers that you feel is unreasonable?
- How easily do you accept constructive criticism?
- Are you willing to ask for help?
- Do you make decisions or judgments with confidence?
- How open are you to another person's suggestions or advice?
- When you state your thoughts or feelings, do you do so in a direct and sincere manner?
- Are you likely to cooperate with others to achieve a worthwhile goal?

Being Assertive

One of the best ways to build confidence is to let people know what you want and don't want, how you feel, and when you need help. The more skilled you are at letting people know these things, the more assertive you'll become. The more you *successfully* assert yourself, the more confident you'll become. So how do you become more assertive? Let's start by assessing where you are right now.

If you answered "yes" to less than half of the questions in the "Assertiveness Check-Up" box above, the strategies below can help you feel more confident when you are attempting to be assertive.

- Use suitable facial expressions.
- Always maintain good eye contact.
- Watch your tone of voice. Your voice should be firm, audible, and pleasant.
- Be aware of your body language — how you stand, sit, and gesture.
- Actively listen to others so that you can accurately confirm what they have said.

- Ask reasoned questions when something is unclear to you.
- Take a win-win approach to solving problems: How can what you're asking for benefit both you and the person you're asking?

Developing a Network

When you create a supportive network of individuals, you are being interdependent, and this is a key to fostering self-confidence. By building mutually helpful relationships, you are more likely to achieve your goals and dreams. Here are some strategies for developing this interdependence:

- Actively seek out your school's many resources. This will mean connecting with an academic advisor, signing up for a tutor if you need one, or getting involved with several on- or off-campus activities.
- Foster a valuable relationship with your instructors; ask for their assistance, feedback, and constructive criticism.
- Start a study group by looking for several classmates who are prepared, regularly attend classes, and take an active part in class discussions. Don't overlook a quiet student who may have true insight into the course; he or she can prove an asset. Approach those you've identified and suggest forming the group. If the answer is yes, decide on your group's mutual goals and the rules your group will follow.
- Coming to college can be a challenging and emotionally stressful experience; fortunately, your school offers counselors who can provide the understanding and skill to help you overcome your issues, so turning to one can be the right thing to do.

Advice from Other Students

The Goal Setter: Liberal Arts Major at the Community College of Rhode Island

Having little idea what he wanted to do upon entering college, the Goal Setter elected to not declare a specific major; instead he chose general education courses to slowly get himself "into the student mind-set." High school had been a struggle academically and personally, so a four-year school was not an immediate option. Previously, his only goal was to not leave school early, and now he realized he needed more structure. He connected with an advisor, and she suggested that he first take a self-assessment test and, based on the results, come up with a set of both short-term and long-term goals. The advisor explained the value in doing such an exercise and cautioned that he not give up before achieving some or all of those goals. The Goal Setter heeded this advice, earned his associate's degree, and has since transferred to a four-year college, full of confidence that his next goal of a bachelor's diploma will be realized.

The Networker: Marketing Major at Bryant University, Rhode Island

Her high school counselor told the Networker that she was "not college material," and she retained that belief until her early thirties, when she decided that she had something to prove to the counselor *and to herself*. She employed interdependence, surrounding herself with students who practiced successful strategies and who regularly encouraged her. The result was a mostly successful first-semester experience. Following this positive outcome, she never looked back, except to wait for the day when she returned to her former high school to display her diploma to her former guidance counselor.

TIPS FOR CONFIDENCE BUILDING

Here are some time-tested strategies that will help you throughout your life. By following these steps, you will achieve *realistic and worthwhile* confidence:

- As often as possible, focus on your strong points rather than areas of weakness. In other words, be aware of what is good about you rather than what you are not proud of.
- Make a consistent effort to learn from your experiences — the good and bad (you will undoubtedly have many of both in your life).
- Find the courage to try something new and different, even when it appears too difficult or risky.
- When something bothers or disappoints you, take the time to examine your thoughts. Choose to react calmly and rationally rather than on impulse and your emotions.
- Expect that while some of what you achieve in life may be due to pure luck, a good deal more will likely be the result of your personal persistence and effort.
- Strive to be assertive. This means express how you feel, what you think, the beliefs you hold, and do so directly and sincerely. You have a right to say "no" to requests that are not genuine or reasonable.
- Continue to learn and vary your skills and talents long after you leave college. Embrace the idea that there is no end to learning throughout your life.
- Most important of all, believe in yourself. Identify what distinguishes you from everyone else and what you have to offer. Once you know these qualities, you will begin to cultivate them by applying them in everyday life.

Managing Your Time

You might be the kind of student who thinks it's normal to spend hours making flashcards and outlining your notes in different colored ink. Or maybe you're an adrenaline junkie, accustomed to starting a twenty-page term paper the night before it's due.

The problem is both of these approaches carry certain inherent liabilities. Goof off and you'll probably bomb all your courses. Do nothing but cower in a library carrel for weeks on end and you'll wind up dull, pasty, and miserable. If you're like most of us, you'll learn more, get better grades, and have more fun in college if you operate somewhere in the middle.

By now, you've probably heard the Latin expression *carpe diem*, which translates to "seize the day" (as in, make time work for you). Mastering the art of time management is one key to your future success and happiness, but learning to actually make time work for you can be problematic. What can you do to take control of your own time? Read on to find out.

The Case for Time Management

Why bother? We know. Some students don't want to "waste" time on planning and managing their schedules. Instead, they prefer to go with the flow. Unfortunately, the demands of college (not to mention most careers) require serious, intentional strategies. Unless you can afford to hire a personal assistant, your previous slacker habits won't carry you through.

To psych yourself up, think of time management as part of your life skill set. If you're trying to remember all the things you need to get done, it's hard to focus on actually doing the work. Organizing your time well accomplishes three things: First, it optimizes your chances for good results, so you're not flying by the seat of your pants. Second, it enhances your life by saving you from stress and regret. And finally, it reflects what you value — it's all about doing your best.

Need more motivation? Remember that people who learn good time-management techniques in college generally soar in their careers. Think about it: If you're more efficient at your job, you'll be able to accomplish more. That will give you a competitive advantage over your coworkers. Your bosses will learn to depend on you. They'll reward you with interesting projects, promotions, and educational and training opportunities. You'll feel empowered and will fill your workplace with positive vibes. You'll have time for a sizzling social life outside the office. Plus you'll make more money and need fewer energy drinks.

Taking Charge of Your Time

Freedom can be a dangerous thing. One of the biggest differences between high school and college is that you find yourself with far more independence — and greater responsibility — than you've ever known. If you are continuing your education after a break, you may also be contending with spouse/boss/child obligations, too. But it would be a gigantic mistake to assume that Oprah, rocket scientists, and other type-A folks have some kind of monopoly on organization and focus. You, the ordinary student, can also embrace your inner executive assistant — the one who keeps you on time, on task, and ready for a slice of the action. So how do you begin?

Setting Goals

Goals help you figure out where to devote the majority of your time. To achieve your goals, you need to do more than just think about them. You need to act! This requires setting some short-term and long-term goals. When determining your long-term goals, it is important to be honest and realistic with yourself. Goals should be challenging, but they should also be attainable. Be sure they align with your abilities, values, and interests. Do you want to go on to further schooling? Have you decided what career you want to pursue? Mulling over these questions can help you start thinking about where you want to be in the next five to ten years. Dreaming up long-term goals can be exciting and fun; however, reaching your goals requires undertaking a number of steps in the short term.

Try to be very specific when determining your short-term goals. For example, if you're committed to becoming an expert in a certain field, you'll want to throw yourself into every class and internship that can help you on your way. A specific goal would be to review your school's course catalog, identify the courses you want to take, and determine when you must take them. An even more specific goal would be to research interesting internship opportunities in your field of study. The good news about goals is that each small step adds up.

Identify one long-term goal and identify three steps you can take to achieve your goal.

Long-Term Goal _____

Steps toward Your Goal

1. _____
2. _____
3. _____

Knowing Your Priorities

To achieve your goals, prioritize your life so that you're steadily working toward them.

- **Start out with a winner's mentality:** Make sure your studies take precedence. Having worked so hard to get to college, you cannot allow other activities to derail your schoolwork. Review your current commitments and prepare to sacrifice a few—for now. Whatever you do, talk to your family, your boss, and your friends about your college workload and goals so that everyone's on the same page. When you have a looming deadline, be firm. Emphasize that no amount of badgering will succeed in getting you to go to the James Bond theme party during finals week.

- **Next, start preparing for your future:** Visit your campus career center and schedule an assessment test to hone in on your talents and interests. Or, if you know what career you want to pursue, talk with a professional in that field, your guidance counselor, a professor, or an upper-class student in your chosen major to find out what steps you need to take to get the results you want, starting now. What skills and experiences should be on your résumé when you graduate that will make you stand out from the pack? Make a plan, prioritize your goals, and then make a time-management schedule.

- **Balance is key:** If you're realistic, planning for the future you want may demand big sacrifices. Be realistic about the present, too. Always include time in your schedule for people who are important to you and time on your own to recharge.

Embrace the Two-for-One Rule. For every hour you spend in class at college, you should plan to study two hours more outside of class. That's the standard, so keep it in mind when you're planning your schedule. The bottom line is that you simply carry more responsibility for your education in college than you did in high school.

Own Your Class Schedule. Your schedule will impact almost every aspect of your college life. Before you register, think about how to make your schedule work for you.

> **TIP**
>
> **Share Your Google or Outlook Calendar.** Keeping an electronic copy of your calendar allows you to share with others at a click of the button. Letting your family, friends, and employer know what is on your plate at any given moment can bridge any misunderstandings that may arise because of your school commitments and may create a more supportive home and work environment.

- **Start with your biorhythms.** Do you study more effectively in the day or the evening or a combination of both? Ideally, you should devote your peak hours—when you're most alert and engaged—to schoolwork. Schedule other activities, like laundry, e-mail, exercise, and socializing, for times when it's harder to concentrate.

- **If you live on campus,** you might want to create a schedule that situates you near a dining hall at mealtimes or lets you spend breaks between classes at the library. Feel free to slot breaks for relaxation and catching up with friends. But beware the midday nap: You risk feeling lethargic afterward or even worse, oversleeping and missing the rest of your classes. If you attend a large college or university, be sure to allow adequate time to get from one class to another.

- **Try to alternate classes with free periods.** Also, seek out instructors who will let you attend lectures at alternate times in case you're absent. If they offer flexibility with due dates for assignments, all the better.

- **If you're a commuter student or carry a heavy workload,** you might be tempted to schedule your classes in blocks without breaks. But before you do this, consider the following:
  - Falling behind in all your classes if you get sick
  - The fatigue factor
  - No last-minute study periods before tests
  - The possibility of having several exams on the same day

CONTROL FACTOR: KNOW WHAT YOU *CAN* AND *CAN'T* CONTROL

When it comes to planning your time between what you can and can't control, it helps to know the difference.

What You *Can* Control

- **Making good choices.** How often do you say, "I don't have time"? Probably a lot. But truth be told, you have a choice when it comes to most of the major commitments in your life. You also control many of the small decisions that keep you focused on your goals: when you wake up, how much sleep you get, what you eat, how much time you spend studying, and whether you get exercise. So be a person with a plan. If you want something enough, you'll make time for it.

- **Doing your part to succeed.** Translation: Go to all your classes; arrive on time; buy all the required textbooks; keep track of your activities; complete every reading and writing assignment on time; take notes in class; and, whenever possible, participate and ask questions.

- **Managing your stress levels.** Organization is the key to tranquility and positive thinking. Manage your time well, and you won't be tormented with thoughts of all the things that need doing. Psychologists have found that free-floating anxiety can turn even your subconscious thoughts into a horror show. Want to avoid unnecessary stress? Plan ahead.

What You *Can't* Control

- **Knowing how much you'll need to study right off the bat.** Depending on the kind of high school you went to (and the types of courses you took there) or if it has been a while since you've had to study, you might be more or less prepared than your college classmates. If your studying or writing skills lag behind, expect to put in a little extra time until you're up to speed.

- **Running into scheduling conflicts.** If you find it hard to get the classes you need, you can seek help from a dean, an academic adviser, or someone in the college counseling center.

- **Needing a job to help pay your way.** Just follow the experts' rule of thumb: If you're taking a full course load, do your best to avoid working more than fifteen hours a week. Any more than that and your academic work could suffer.

Four Time-Wasting Habits to Avoid

1. Procrastinating

Should you have to do assignments that seem incredibly long and boring? Shouldn't you be able to study with family members in the room, even if you can't get any work done with them around? Can't you occasionally blow off the outside reading? Yes, no, and no.

There are lots of reasons why we procrastinate. Maybe you're a perfectionist — in which case, avoiding a task might be easier than having to live up to your own very high expectations (or those of your parents or instructors). Maybe you object to the sheer dullness of an assignment, or you think you can learn the material just as well without doing the work. Maybe you even fear success and know just how to subvert it.

None of these qualify as valid reasons to put off your work. They're just excuses that will get you in trouble. Fortunately, doing tasks you don't like is excellent practice for real life.

Slacker alert: Procrastination is a slippery slope. Research shows that procrastinators are more likely to develop unhealthy habits like higher alcohol consumption, smoking, insomnia, poor diet, and lack of exercise. Make sure you get these tendencies under control early. Otherwise, you could feel overwhelmed in other aspects of your life, too.

> **EASY TRICKS TO STOP PROCRASTINATION**
>
> - **Break big jobs down into smaller chunks.** Spend only a few minutes planning your strategy and then act on it.
> - **Reward yourself** for finishing the task, like watching your favorite YouTuber or playing a game with your kids or friends.
> - **Find a quiet, comfortable place to work** that doesn't allow for distractions and interruptions. Don't listen to music, and turn off your phone. If you study in your room, shut the door.
> - **Treat your study time like a serious commitment.** That means no phone calls, e-mail, text messages, or updates to your Facebook page. You can rejoin society later.
> - **Consider the consequences if you don't get down to work.** You don't want to let bad habits derail your ability to achieve good results *and* have a life.

2. Overextending Yourself

Feeling overextended is a huge source of stress for college students. Why? Well, what constitutes a realistic workload varies significantly from one person to another. Being involved in campus life is fun and important, but it's crucial not to let your academic work take a backseat.

- **Learn to say no — even if it means letting other people down.** Don't be tempted to compromise your priorities.

- **But don't give up all nonacademic pursuits.** On the contrary, students who work or participate in extracurricular activities often achieve higher grades than their less-active counterparts partly because of the important role that time management plays in their lives.
- **If you're truly overloaded with commitments and can't see a way out . . .** you may need to drop a course before the drop deadline. It may seem drastic, but a low grade on your permanent record is even worse. Become familiar with your school's add/drop policy to avoid penalties. If you receive financial aid, keep in mind that in most cases you must be registered for a minimum number of credit hours to be considered a full-time student and maintain your current level of aid. Be sure before you drop!

3. Losing Your Focus

Too many first-year college students lose sight of their goals. Translation: They spend their first term blowing off classes and assignments, then either get expelled, placed on probation, or have to spend years clawing their way back to a decent GPA. So plan your strategy and keep yourself motivated for the long haul.

4. Running Late

Punctuality is a virtue. Rolling in late to class or review sessions shows a lack of respect for both your instructors and your classmates. Arrive early and avoid using your phone in class, texting, doing homework for another class, falling asleep, talking, whispering, or leaving class to feed a parking meter. Part of managing your time is freeing yourself to focus on the present and on other people who inhabit the present with you. Note: Respecting others is a habit that can work wonders in your career and personal life.

> **TIP**
>
> **Social Media Addict?** Online tools like *StayFocused* allow you to block or limit your time on certain Web sites while you are studying so you can focus on the task at hand. Google "10 Online Tools for Better Attention & Focus" to find a program that works for you.

Two Indispensable Tools to Keep You on Track

Here's the deal. Once you enter college or the working world, you must immediately do the following: Write down everything you need to do; prioritize your tasks; and leave yourself constant reminders. The good news is that a little up-front planning will make your life infinitely easier and more relaxing. For one thing, you'll be less likely to screw up. On top of that, you'll free your brain from having to remember all the things you need to get done so you can focus on actually doing the work. Two key items will help you plan to succeed.

A Planner or Calendar

Find out if your college sells a special planner in the campus bookstore with important dates and deadlines already marked. Or, if you prefer to use an online calendar or the one that comes on your computer or smartphone, that's fine too. As you schedule your time, follow a few basic guidelines.

Pick a timeframe that works best for you. If you want a "big picture" sense of how your schedule plays out, try setting up a calendar for the whole term or for the month. For a more detailed breakdown of what you need to accomplish in the near future, a calendar for the week or even the day may be a better fit. Of course, there's no need to limit yourself—use more than one type of calendar if that works for you.

Enter all of your commitments. Once you've selected your preferred timeframe, it's time to record your commitments and other important deadlines. These might include your classes, assignment due dates, work hours, family commitments, and so on. Be specific. For instance, "Read Chapter 8 in history" is preferable to "Study history," which is better than simply "Study." To be even more specific, include meeting times and locations, social events, and study time for each class you're taking. Take advantage of your smartphone and set reminders and alarms to help keep you on top of all your activities and obligations.

Break large assignments like term papers into smaller bits, such as choosing a topic, doing research, creating an outline, learning necessary computer skills, writing a first draft, and so on. And give them deadlines. Estimate how much time each assignment will take you. Then get a jump on it. A good time manager often finishes projects before the actual due dates to allow for emergencies.

Watch out for your toughest weeks during the term. If you find that paper deadlines and test dates fall during the same week or even the same day, you can alleviate some of the stress by finding time to finish some assignments early to free up study and writing time. If there's a major conflict, talk it over with your professor and find a way to work around it. Professors will be more likely to help you if you come to them plenty of time in advance.

Update your planner/calendar regularly. Enter all due dates as soon as you know them. Be obsessive about this.

Check your planner/calendar every day (at the same time of day if that helps you remember). You'll want to review the current week and the next week, too.

When in doubt, turn to a type-A classmate for advice. A hyper-organized friend can be your biggest ally when it comes to making a game plan.

A To-Do List

The easiest way to remember all the things you need to do is to jot them down in a running to-do list—updating as needed. You can do this on paper or use an online calendar or smartphone to record the day's obligations. Techies love the GTD® ("Getting Things Done"®) system for taking control of tasks and commitments. Google it to learn how it works.

1. **Prioritize.** Rank items on your list in order of importance. Alternately, circle or highlight urgent tasks. Exclamation points and stars—it's all good.
2. **Every time you complete a task, cross it off the list.** (This can be extremely satisfying.)
3. **Move undone items to the top of your next list.** (Less satisfying, but smart and efficient.)

4. **Start a new to-do list every day or once a week.** It shouldn't be just about academics. Slot in errands you need to run, appointments, e-mail messages you need to send, and anything else you need to do that day or week.

Advice from Other Students

Martha Flot
Education Major in Florida

"I learned a long time ago that if I don't start my work early, it's not going to happen. I always open my books right after the kids are off to school and begin with the easiest assignments. I feel really productive and get into the swing of things before tackling the harder stuff. It's kind of like the warm-up before practice."

- **Digitally bolster your memory.** "I keep everything in my smartphone calendar—for me, that's the best way to stay organized. I set reminders for all of my study groups and upcoming assignments. If it's a big exam, I'll set the reminder a week in advance to give myself plenty of time to prepare."

- **Exercise.** "I always try to exercise before I sit down for an exam or a long study session, too. Studies show that exercise boosts your blood circulation, so you can think better and feel more awake. For me, it makes a huge difference."

- **Beware of overcommitting.** "I used to be a huge people pleaser. Trying to please everyone and juggling my role as a mother, wife, and student, I learned fast that I couldn't do that and still get all my work done. Once I started prioritizing, my friends and family have been responsive and supportive. It helps having a husband who manages his time well; you grow and learn from it."

EASY WAYS TO MAXIMIZE YOUR TIME

- **Carry work with you.** If you have a lull between classes, use it to review material from the previous class and prepare for the next one. Take advantage of waiting time (on the bus or between appointments) to study. You'll be more likely to remember what you've learned in class if you review or copy your notes as soon as you reasonably can.
- **Discipline yourself with routines.** You might want to get up early to prepare, or set fixed study hours after dinner or on weekend afternoons.
- **Don't multitask.** Even though you might be quite good at it, or think you are, the reality is—and research shows—that you'll be able to do your most effective studying and retain the most information if you concentrate on one task at a time.
- **Study with friends.** You can help each other grasp tricky concepts and memorize important facts and dates.
- **Be flexible.** Disruptions to your plans don't come with ample warning time. Build extra time into your schedule so that unanticipated interruptions don't prevent you from meeting your goals.

John Dietz
Architecture Major in Florida

"My first two years of college forced me to be a morning person. But as an upperclassman, I have the freedom to pick classes that start in the afternoon, so I've reverted to being nocturnal: I usually study or work in my design studio until 2 or 3 a.m."

- **Go digital.** "I take my computer to all my classes, so I keep a detailed calendar there. My work schedule changes frequently, so I always type that in along with all my assignments."

- **Beware of perfectionism.** "As an architect, you could spend your whole life designing something. Often I really have to tell myself to stop and go on to the next thing."

- **Find a part-time job that offers flexible hours and lets you study.** "I work at the gym on campus, where each shift is just three hours long. They only hire students, so they're very accommodating if I need to change my schedule. Plus, mostly I get to sit at the check-in desk and review my notes."

Carolina Buckler
Business and Political Science Major in Indiana

"Having a double major means a heavier workload, but it's doable in my subjects. My roommate — who's studying engineering and puts in a lot more hours than I do — couldn't have handled a heavier workload because of his major."

- **Start things sooner rather than later.** "That especially helps with group projects because it's hard to find time in everyone's schedule to get together. If you meet early, you can divide up the work."

- **Make sure your employer knows your academic commitments.** "I work twelve to fifteen hours a week as a teacher's assistant in the political science department. The professors will automatically understand if I need to take a study day. Around finals, they give everyone a week off."

- **Socialize at mealtimes.** "My friends and I meet for dinner at 5 p.m. It sounds ridiculously early, but I've found that it makes me less likely to waste time: Instead of trying to start something for an hour or so before dinner, I get back around 6:30 and jump right into homework."

3

Writing Ethically and Responsibly

Thanks to technology, it's easier than ever for students to cheat — so cheaters are sprouting like mushrooms. Thanks to technology, it's also much easier for colleges to catch cheaters. And administrators are cracking down on cheating by making the penalties increasingly harsh.

To complicate matters, there are plenty of students who cheat *without even knowing that they're cheating*. Of course, in a perfect world, they'd get lighter sentences than the people who cheated intentionally. But colleges aren't perfect worlds. They're wonderful institutions of learning that don't like to be taken advantage of.

So let's clear a few things up.

Defining "Cheating"

Cheating comes down to two things: Faking your own work and helping other students fake theirs.

Some of the Most Obvious Forms of Cheating

- Buying an essay from someone else
- Texting answers during an exam
- Sharing the details of a test with students who haven't taken it yet
- Copying someone else's homework
- Peeking at someone else's test paper
- Letting other people cheat off you
- Stealing a test
- Writing answers to the test in crazy small letters on your gum wrappers or on the inside of your bottled water label (Note: Professors are onto these tricks.)
- Plagiarizing: the most common (but equally problematic) form of cheating

The trouble with plagiarism is that a lot of students don't completely understand what it is. Plagiarism is a fancy word that, according to the *Oxford English Dictionary*, means "taking someone else's work or ideas and passing them off as one's own." Fun fact: The word *plagiarism* comes from the Latin word for *kidnapping*.

It's hard to believe that anybody *really* thinks it's okay to cut and paste whole sentences from the Internet into their essays. But given that some people don't think twice about downloading copyrighted music tracks and videos, maybe the concept of "borrowing" isn't as clear as it used to be. What's your stance? Have you ever lifted passages off a website, maybe even changing a couple of words to make it sound more like you? Are you inclined to believe that once something is on the Web, it's public domain? If so, please know it's *not* so. The fact remains that copying or paraphrasing anything off the Internet (or from any another source) and using it without citing the source is cheating.

Beware: Plagiarizing with intent is one thing. But many college students who plagiarize by accident — they copy quotations into their notes but forget to add quotation marks and later can't tell what's their own writing and what they borrowed from a source — are also convicted of plagiarism simply because they forgot to indicate which parts of an essay are their own and which parts belong to another author. We repeat: Colleges are on a crusade to thwart cheating. If your high school was lax about footnotes or paraphrasing, you need to figure out the rules fast.

The Cheating Problem

In a recent survey of 36,000 high school students by the Josephson Institute of Ethics, 60 percent admitted to cheating on a test during the previous year. Thirty-five percent had cheated on multiple tests. A third of them had committed plagiarism, cutting and pasting from the Internet. What's worse, according to studies by Donald L. McCabe at Rutgers University, the number of students who think that copying material from the Web is "serious cheating" has plummeted to only 29 percent.

Cheating typically begins during junior high, which is — no surprise — around the same time that grade pressure and academic workloads ramp up. In college, the pressure to get good grades becomes even more intense. Maybe you're trying to get into a competitive graduate program, win a scholarship, or land a high-paying job. Maybe you're involved in a zillion clubs, sports, or volunteer activities. Maybe you have a job and/or kids. Maybe you're taking metaphysics. Whatever it is, you could start to feel overextended. And from there, you might start to justify cheating in your mind. Big mistake.

Why You Shouldn't Cheat

Because it's wrong. Because getting caught could set off a firestorm and totally screw up your future. Because cheating is bad for your self-image and can trigger severe guilt and anxiety.

Because attending college is ultimately about learning new things, challenging yourself, and building your integrity. If you try to scam your way through, you've defeated the whole point of this exercise.

And here's the real drag: Cheating has a nasty way of seeping into other parts of your life, like your career, your finances, and your personal relationships, where it can cause long-term damage. Once you've cheated on a few tests, it might not seem like a big leap for you to start padding your résumé or fudging your taxes.

Why It's Easy to Get Caught

College professors have more time and leeway to investigate their suspicions and better resources to back them up. Programs like Turnitin.com let instructors scan essays and crosscheck them against books, newspapers, journals, and student papers, as well as against material that's publicly accessible on the Web. Even a tiny, nine-word snippet could give you away.

How *Not* to Cheat: Ten Essential Tips

1. **Avoid friends who pressure you to bend the rules.** Writing a paper is really hard. Doing advanced math and science homework is really hard. Studying for exams is lonely, boring, and *really* hard. But trying to beat the system doesn't pay. Remind yourself of the consequences of cheating. Explain to your friends that you are on a valiant quest for honest effort. Make them watch a lot of movies about Abraham Lincoln. As a last resort, find new friends.

2. **Join a study group.** If you're struggling to get through a daunting course, get together with other students to compare notes and help each other grasp tricky concepts. A study group gives you a support system and a more positive belief in yourself. It teaches you persistence and discipline because the group

---

THE PENALTIES FOR CHEATING

Cheating is a much bigger deal in college than it was in high school. Remember, you're not a minor anymore. Once you're over 18 and are caught cheating, you'll be reprimanded as an adult.

- "At minimum, you're looking at an F for the entire course and very likely academic probation or even dismissal," says Dr. Thomas Skouras, a professor at the Community College of Rhode Island. "In most cases now, instructors have to adhere to the school's policy on cheating, so they can't bend the rules even if they want to."
- And it gets scarier than that: If caught cheating, you could end up with a Conviction of Plagiarism on your college transcript. That's the same transcript you'll need to use for graduate school and job applications.
- Plagiarism is different from other student offenses in that it isn't protected under federal confidentiality laws. Think about it: "A student who has stalked someone on campus and has a history of psychiatric illness might not have that information on his transcript," Prof. Skouras adds. "A conviction of cheating is much harder to suppress."

Note: How often are convictions of plagiarism overturned? Almost never. Most instructors won't go forward with the charges unless they have substantial evidence to back them up.

structure involves meeting promptly at set times for reviews. A study group can also make learning easier and more fun. Other members of the group may have noticed important points from class that you didn't catch. Plus, once you understand the material well, any impulse to cheat will cease to be an issue.

> **TIP**
>
> **Make a pledge to successfully pass the course as a team—the honest way.** "I chose to form a group more than a decade ago with three other doctoral candidates, and we followed through on our promise to graduate together," says Prof. Skouras. "It really mattered that we were each rooting for the others to succeed."

3. **Don't procrastinate.** Here's the deal: If you want to write a thorough and honest essay, you need to start early. College papers aren't like movie reviews. You're required to do lots of outside research. Then you have to weed through it all to figure out what's valuable. Next, you have to incorporate the highlights into an outline, a first draft, and ultimately, an original, dazzlingly brilliant work that's all your own. All of that takes time. If you leave things too late, you'll be more tempted to cheat.

4. **Don't muddle your notes.** It's vital that you keep your own writing separate from the material you've gathered from other sources. Why? Because it's surprisingly easy to mistake someone else's words for your own, especially after you get two hours into writing and your brain turns numb. So document everything. Be obsessive about this.

5. **Be a stickler for in-text citations.** It happens all the time: At the end of an essay, a student provides a full listing of all the works he or she has cited. But in the paper itself, there are no references to be found. "In this case, you're looking at a low C at best," says Prof. Skouras. "Your instructor has no choice but to take off major points since it's impossible to tell the difference between your writing and your references."

> **TIP**
>
> **Respect deadlines.** When you were in high school, your teachers might have negotiated due dates. In college, it's almost impossible to get an extension on an assignment. Your old stalling tactics ("My printer broke/I have the flu/I've been working with NASA on a nuclear laser shield—so can I get that essay to you on Monday?") won't fly.

6. **Familiarize yourself with the proper formatting for a research paper.** The MLA and APA styles are pretty standard. If your instructors require a different style, they will let you know. If you need to learn the basic guidelines and rules for citations, consult a handbook. The Owl at Purdue University is a great resource—well written and user-friendly (**http://owl.purdue.edu**). You might also want to speak to a reference librarian. A reference librarian has a graduate degree in gathering research and can be one of your biggest allies in college. Alternately, pay a visit to the writing center on campus or talk to your instructor for advice. Many college libraries offer tutorials in MLA formatting. Getting one early in the semester can give you a big leg up.

> **TIP**
>
> **Flaunt your knowledge.** You must not only list the references you've used to research your topic, but you must also demonstrate that you know where they belong in your narrative.

7. **Be sure to list all of your research sources.** If you're not sure how to list a citation or if you're not sure that your source is valid, don't just put it down and keep your fingers crossed. Talk to your instructor, or ask a reference librarian for help.

8. **Master the art of paraphrasing.** Paraphrasing means restating someone else's ideas or observations in your own words and sentences. You don't have to put the text in quotation marks, but a citation acknowledging the original source is still needed. (See *The Rules of Paraphrasing* below for examples.)

9. **If you need help, seek it early.** This sounds painfully obvious, but it's important to go to the writing center or the librarian *well before your paper is actually due*. Revision takes time and, chances are, your paper will need more than a few tweaks.

10. **If you hand something in and then realize that you used material without giving credit to the source, alert your instructor immediately.** Don't just hope it will slip through. Better to risk half a grade on one essay than your whole college career, right?

> **TIP**
>
> **When copying research material into your notes, write the name of its source and page number directly after it.** Likewise, when you copy something from the Internet, add a URL in brackets at the end. Use quotation marks around all cited materials. You might also try highlighting your research in a bright color to set it apart from your notes. All of this will make things easier when it's time to make your footnotes.

The Rules of Paraphrasing

Paraphrasing doesn't mean copying a quote and swapping out a few words. It doesn't mean changing two or three words in a sequence, either. It means rephrasing someone else's quote altogether while retaining its essential meaning. Consider these examples:

- If the quote is "The likelihood of an increase in the growth rate appears dim," you might change it to "The economy improving in the near future is improbable, according to Dr. X, an economist at the University of Y."

- Likewise, "Google has been working to build cars that can drive themselves," could be rewritten as "One of Google's latest projects: a robotic car that takes humans out of the driver's seat."

If you're having trouble paraphrasing something, try this trick: Put away your source material, call up a friend or your mom, and explain the point you're trying to summarize. Chances are you'll come away with something that's clear, concise, and in your own words.

A word of warning: When you paraphrase someone else's opinions or insights, you still have to document the source. The upside? You don't have to frame the passage in quotation marks.

PART TWO

Writing Activities

- **4** Recalling and Observing 27
- **5** Interviewing for Information 32
- **6** Comparing and Contrasting 36
- **7** Explaining Causes and Effects 42
- **8** Taking a Stand 46
- **9** Proposing a Solution 51
- **10** Evaluating and Reviewing 54
- **11** Supporting a Position with Sources 57
- **12** Responding to Literature 61
- **13** Responding to Visual Representations 65

4

Recalling and Observing

Recalling and observing are opportunities for you to write about a personal experience or an interesting scene. Some writers focus on recalling memories, whereas others look around and write based on what they observe. In both recalling and observing, writers provide concrete details to make a point clear or an image or description convincing. You can start by considering these questions:

1. What is recalling?
2. What is observing?
3. Why might recalling and observing make a piece of writing more interesting for the reader?

Pre-assignment Questions

Think about what you have learned about recalling and observing from your instructor and your textbook. After responding to the questions that follow, ask your instructor, a tutor, or a peer to help you answer any questions you still have.

1. Have you ever used writing to recall an experience or observe a scene? If so, what was your writing about? Did you enjoy the process? If you have never written to recall or observe before, you can write about a time when you had a conversation in which you recalled an important incident in your life or observed a scene in detail. Perhaps it was about a moment of triumph, or perhaps it was about a surprising turn of events. What did you say about that moment, and what did you learn from it?
2. How do you feel about recalling or observing in your writing? Are you worried about the process? Excited? Explain why you feel the way you do. If you have concerns, consider discussing them with a peer or your instructor.

3. Being proactive means anticipating challenges so that they don't get in your way. How can you proactively address anything that might get in the way of you writing an awesome essay? For example, if you struggle with procrastination, you might create a schedule that makes time for every step of your work. If you struggle with writing clear or varied sentences, you might do some practice exercises in the "Additional Tools for Practice" section of this workbook.

Understanding Your Assignment

If your instructor has given an assignment that requires you to write an essay that recalls an experience or observes a scene, make sure you understand your assignment before you get started. If your instructor gave you a choice of assignments, first select which assignment you are interested in completing. Read your assignment carefully and answer the questions that follow.

1. Based on the assignment you were given, what type of writing to reflect are you being asked to write? Are you writing from recollection or are you writing from an observation?

2. Write down any words or concepts that you do not understand from the assignment. Consult your textbook or talk with your instructor for clarification. Skip this question if all the words and concepts are clear to you.

3. In your own words, in a way that is most understandable to you, retell what your instructor is asking you to do. Put any special requirements, as broad as topic suggestions and as narrow as font-size requirements, in your assignment retelling. Make sure what you write reflects what you have to do in the assignment by comparing what you wrote to the instructor's assignment several times.

4. If possible, compare your retelling of the assignment to that of another classmate. If your work reveals different understandings of the assignment, look up words and concepts together. If you both still have a different understanding, ask your instructor to clarify the assignment.

How to Write an Observation

Have you ever wanted to share your own ideas based on your observations that might be interesting or even instructive to others? Writing from observation allows you to open all your senses so that you see, smell, taste, hear, and feel. Your purpose is not only to describe an observation but also to express thoughts and feelings connected with what you observe.

What makes writing from observation unique? Think about what you have learned in class as well as your textbook reading before completing the next activities.

Below is a list of steps that will help you gather ideas and draft your essay.

1. Generate ideas.

Activity: Observations start with a place, a group of people, or a scene you want to write about. What places interest you?

Activity: Make a list of potential scenes for you to observe. Possibilities include places where people gather for specific activities or performances (a gym, a classroom, a theater), for special events (a stadium, a place of worship, a community hall), or to travel (a train or bus station, an airport). Write down as many ideas as you can.

2. Ask the "five W's and an H."

Activity: For each item in your list, try asking "the five W's and an H," the questions that reporters ask to gather information. *Who* was involved? *What* happened? *Where* did it take place? *When* did it happen? *Why* did it happen? *How* did the events unfold? Then, consider which of the observations would be most interesting to others, especially readers who do not know you personally. Choose that as your topic for the essay.

3. Identify your purpose and audience.

Activity: Do you want to use your observations to persuade, inform, entertain, or something else? Picture your readers. What do you need to tell them?

4. List relevant observations.

Activity: You can't record everything you observe. You must be selective based on what is important and relevant for your purpose and audience and which details convey the greatest impact. Work on an interesting "hook" to capture the interest of the reader. It may be a scene-setter, such as a description of something or someone, or a quotation, or a brief anecdote to set the background. Good writers work to engage their audience right from the very start.

5. Consider sources of support.

Activity: To confirm some of the information in your writing, you may want to double-check your observations. Depending on how recent your observations are, you can check them against published sources, such as news articles, reports, or even photographs of the person/people, place, or scene that is your subject, or against other eyewitness accounts.

6. Sketch an outline.

Activity: Make a rough outline of your observations. Think in terms of where in your essay you intend to use which specific details. Map them out in a way that conveys the main impression you want to create for your audience. Add transitions that mark place or direction—words or phrases to guide the reader from one vantage point, location, or idea to the next.

7. Draft your essay.

Activity: Ask yourself: What do you want the reader to think or feel by the end of your essay? The answer may involve an attempt to look at something old in a new way, or it may be an appeal to action, or even a prediction for the future. Write down what you want the take-away to be. With that in mind, you can complete your first draft.

8. Revise based on feedback.

Activity: Have others — either fellow students, tutors, or your instructor — read a draft of your essay. Do your readers "get" the feelings and ideas that you're attempting to express, or do they become lost, confused, or even bored? Revise your essay based on the feedback you receive from your readers.

How to Write from Recollection

Writing from recollection allows you to share your own memories of a personal experience that might be interesting or even instructive to others. It is an opportunity to deeply consider what you may have experienced or learned and convey those reflections to your readers. Ideally, your readers will come away having learned or felt something new about your subject or even about you. Your purpose is not merely to tell an interesting story but to show your readers the importance of that experience for you.

What makes writing from recollection unique? Think about what you have learned in class as well as your textbook reading before you complete the next activities.

Below is a list of steps that will help you gather ideas and draft your essay.

1. Generate ideas.

Activity: When you are generating ideas, you write down as many ideas as you can. Start by making a list of events that have had a strong emotional effect on you. It may take time for your memories to surface. Have you ever spoken out against a rule or rebelled against authority? Have you ever given in to peer pressure? Have you ever taken a risk or tried something completely new? What did you learn from your experiences? It may help to focus on a recent event, rather than one in the distant past. Do not be afraid to make the long list. Pick an event that is not too personal, too subjective, or too big to convey effectively to others.

2. Use the "five W's and H" trick.

Activity: For each item on your list, try asking "the five W's and an H," the questions that reporters ask to gather information. *Who* was involved? *What* happened? *Where* did it take place? *When* did it happen? *Why* did it happen? *How* did the events unfold? Record all the details you can recall about your subject — the people, sounds, conversations, locations, and related physical details. Then consider which events would be most interesting to others, especially readers who do not know you personally. Choose that as your topic for the essay.

3. Identify your purpose and audience.

Activity: Do you want to use your memories to persuade, inform, entertain, or something else? Picture your readers. What do you need to tell them about the experience you are describing?

4. List relevant memories.

Activity: You can't record everything you recall about an event or experience. You must be selective based on what's important and relevant for your purpose and audience. Think about what you most want to tell your audience about the experience you are recalling. List memories and details that help the experience come alive for your audience. Good writers work to engage their audience right from the very start.

5. Consider sources of support.

Activity: Because our minds both retain and drop details, you may want to double-check your recollections of an experience. Did you keep a journal at the time? Do your memories match those of a friend or relative who was there? Was it a public event that was in the news?

6. Sketch an outline.

Activity: Make a rough outline of your recollection. You can either establish the chronology of your story or tell it through flashbacks. You may want to start your story in the middle and then, through flashbacks, fill in whatever background a reader needs to know. Whatever your choice, add transitions that mark place or direction — words or phrases to guide the reader from one vantage point, location, or idea to the next.

7. Draft your essay.

Activity: Writing from recollection involves not only describing your experience but giving your readers a sense of why that experience was important. Ask yourself: What effect did the experience have on you? How did it impact you or your thinking? The answer may involve an attempt to look at something old in a new way, or it may be an appeal to action, or even a prediction for the future. Write down what you want the take-away to be. With that in mind, you can complete your first draft.

8. Revise based on feedback.

Activity: Have others — either fellow students, tutors, or your instructor — read a draft of your essay. Do your readers "get" the feelings and ideas that you're attempting to express, or do they become lost, confused, or even bored? Revise your essay based on the feedback you receive from your readers.

5

Interviewing for Information

We ask others for information all the time. For example, you might ask a friend what she or he thinks of a particular class, movie, or restaurant to find out if it's worth your time and money. The main differences between a casual request for information and an interview are planning and depth. In an interview, you ask questions designed to draw out specific information to get to know other people, understand their perspectives, and discover what they know. An interviewee can be a friend, family member, or coworker. Often it is someone you do not know who has expertise in an area of interest. For example, you might get detailed information about a college major you're interested in by interviewing a professor who teaches in that field. Sometimes the interview becomes the subject of an entire essay. Other times, the interview is just one source of many that you can draw on to support your ideas. To start thinking about interviews, consider the following questions:

1. What are the benefits of conducting an interview?
2. How does information from an interview differ from information you might find in a book or journal?
3. Why might you want to include quotations from an interview in your writing?

Pre-assignment Questions

Think about what you have learned about writing an essay based on an interview from your instructor and your textbook. After responding to the questions that follow, ask your instructor, a tutor, or a peer to help you answer any questions you still have.

1. Have you conducted an interview before? If so, whom did you interview? What did you learn from the interviewee? Did you enjoy thinking and writing about what you learned? If you have never conducted an interview, think of an informative casual conversation you had recently and answer the same questions.

2. How do you feel about writing this essay? Are you worried about the process? Excited? Explain why you feel the way you do. If you have concerns, consider discussing them with a peer or your instructor.

3. Being proactive means anticipating challenges so that they don't get in your way. How can you proactively address anything that might get in the way of you writing an awesome essay? For example, if you struggle with procrastination, you might create a schedule that makes time for every step of your work. If you struggle with paraphrasing another person's words, think of a proactive step that might help you successfully conduct an interview and write about it. If you struggle with writing clear or varied sentences, you might do some practice exercises in the "Additional Tools for Practice" section of this workbook.

Understanding Your Assignment

Make sure you understand your assignment before you get started. If your instructor gave you a choice of assignments, first select which assignment you are interested in completing. Read your assignment carefully and answer the questions that follow.

1. Write any words or concepts that you do not understand from the assignment. Consult your textbook or talk with your instructor for clarification. Skip this question if all the words and concepts are clear to you.

2. In your own words, in a way that is most understandable to you, retell what your instructor is asking you to do. Make sure your assignment retelling includes all requirements of the original assignment. Compare your retelling with the instructor's original assignment several times to make sure that what you've written is complete and accurate.

3. If possible, compare your retelling of the assignment to that of another classmate. If your work reveals different understandings of the assignment, look up words and concepts together. If you both still have a different understanding, ask your instructor to clarify the assignment.

4. Identify passages in your textbook and course materials that address conducting and writing about interviews. Be sure to refer to these resources as you consider your assignment and begin to write. If you have questions about them, ask your instructor.

How to Write an Essay Based on an Interview

An interview is a planned conversation with a purpose. Responding to the steps that follow will help you have a successful interview and share what you learn with your readers. Keep in mind what you have learned in class as well as from your textbook reading as you complete these steps.

What makes writing based on an interview unique? Think about what you have learned in class as well as your textbook reading before completing the next activities.

Below is a list of steps that will help you gather ideas and draft your essay.

1. Identify your interviewee.

Activity: Based on the requirements of your assignment and your own areas of interest, think about who you might interview. What topic would you discuss with that person? What do you want to learn from them, and what do you want to teach your readers about? To have plenty of material for your assignment, make sure your interviewee is someone with enough knowledge and experience to answer your questions in a thoughtful, detailed way.

2. Contact your interviewee.

Activity: Especially if your interviewee is someone you don't know well, it's a good idea to ask that person ahead of time if she or he is willing to participate in an interview. Give your interviewee a sense of when the interview will happen and how long it might take. Making sure a specific person is available to participate will help the process go smoothly, and having a specific person in mind may affect the questions you draft.

3. Conduct additional research, if needed.

Activity: Is your interviewee the only source of information for your assignment? If your assignment requires other sources, such as books or journals, identify sources that will provide useful background or support for your writing. Taking a look through them before conducting your interview may help you develop additional specific questions for your interviewee.

4. Draft and revise interview questions.

Activity: To get detailed responses, avoid questions that can be answered with a simple "Yes" or "No." In general, effective questions being with *Who? What? Where? When?* or *How?* Try to focus your questions on what genuinely interests or confuses you. Make sure your questions are respectful and not too personal. Ask peers or a tutor to review your draft questions; they might help you think of additional questions or raise concerns about questions that might be ineffective.

5. Share questions with your interviewee ahead of time.

Activity: If your interviewee has your prepared questions in advance, they have time to get comfortable with them and think about the best way to respond.

6. Conduct your interview.

Activity: Find out if your interviewee is willing to have the session audio recorded. Having a recording of the interview can help you double check your notes and fill in any blanks later on. During the conversation, try to be flexible. If your interviewee says something that inspires a new question, something you didn't include in your prepared interview, go ahead and ask. Spontaneous follow-up questions show that you are interested and engaged. Sometimes an interviewee will need time to form a response. If the interviewee seems to be comfortably mulling over what to say, be patient. However, if your interviewee seems uncomfortable with a question or is unable to answer, try to steer the conversation in a different direction. Take notes during the interview. They will be helpful to you as you draft your essay.

Be observant during the interview. Spend a little time observing and making notes about physical details. Try to describe the setting of the interview, whether it is a room in a house, an office, or a public meeting space. What is the interviewee wearing? Can you describe her or his posture and attitude?

7. Evaluate your notes and draft a thesis statement.

Activity: After conducting your interview, read through your notes. What stands out to you? Are there specific details or phrases that seem particularly meaningful or memorable? What did you learn from your interviewee? What do you want your readers to learn from your interview and your writing about it? Draft a thesis statement that captures what you want to convey about your subject. Your thesis statement should be supported by your interview and any other sources you might have consulted.

8. Make an outline.

Activity: Now that you have decided what you want your readers to understand about your topic and what information you need to share with them, think of a way to organize your thoughts so that your readers can follow them. For example, if your interviewee holds a job you're interested in, you might group their responses into categories and devote a paragraph to each one: *Becoming interested in the field, Becoming educated in the field, Acquiring a job in the field, Learning from the job.*

9. Draft your paper.

Activity: Using your outline as a guide, draft paragraphs to flesh out your ideas about your topic, and support those ideas with details from your interview. To help orient your readers, you may want to provide background information about your interviewee. Include your thesis statement, so that readers understand what you intend to say and why it matters.

If your assignment requires other sources, be sure to draw on them for support. You will need to decide when to paraphrase and when to directly quote what your interviewee said. In many cases, the interviewee's own words will be most interesting to you and your readers, but paraphrasing will help when you need to capture the heart of a rambling response or state in plain terms a response that included language your readers are not familiar with. Make sure all quotations are accurate. If you do not have a recording and you are unsure of the accuracy of your notes, you can ask your interviewee to confirm specific quotations. Although paraphrase relies on your own words, make sure it fairly and accurately reflects what your interviewee said.

6

Comparing and Contrasting

A comparison and contrast essay analyzes the similarities and differences between two objects, activities, places, people, or other comparable things. When you compare, you point out similarities; when you contrast, you discuss differences. When you write about two complicated subjects, usually you need to do both. Instead of concluding that one subject is great and the other inferior, you might conclude that they are each distinct with individual characteristics. On the other hand, if your main purpose is to judge between two subjects, you would look especially for positive and negative features, weigh their attractions and faults, and then make your choice. Drawing comparisons and identifying contrasts in the world around you is important in many contexts. You can start by considering these questions:

1. What does it mean to compare and contrast?
2. What is the difference between comparing and contrasting?

Pre-assignment Questions

Think about what you have learned about comparing and contrasting from your instructor and your textbook. After responding to the questions that follow, ask your instructor, a tutor, or a peer to help you answer any questions you still have.

1. Have you written a comparison and contrast essay before? If so, what was it about? Did you enjoy the process? If you have never written a comparison and contrast essay before, talk about a verbal comparison you have given to someone.
2. How do you feel about writing this essay? Are you worried about the process? Excited? Explain why you feel the way you do. If you have concerns, consider discussing them with a peer or your instructor.
3. Being proactive means anticipating challenges so that they don't get in your way. How can you proactively address anything that might get in the way of

you writing an awesome essay? For example, if you struggle with procrastination, you might create a schedule that makes time for every step of your work. If you struggle with writing clear or varied sentences, you might do some practice exercises in the "Additional Tools for Practice" section of this workbook.

Understanding Your Assignment

Make sure you understand your assignment before you get started. If your instructor gave you a choice of assignments, first select which assignment you are interested in completing. Read your assignment carefully and answer the questions that follow.

1. Based on the assignment that you were given, what type of comparison and contrast essay are you being asked to write? Is it a source-based assignment or a visual assignment? Are you collaborating with a small group or writing by yourself? Are you writing a comparison and contrast essay to make a decision about something or to show why one subject is better than another?

2. Write down any words or concepts that you do not understand from the assignment. Consult your textbook or talk with your instructor for clarification. Skip this question if all the words and concepts are clear to you.

3. In your own words, in a way that is most understandable to you, retell what your instructor is asking you to do. Put any special requirements, as broad as topic suggestions and as narrow as font-size requirements, in your assignment retelling. Make sure what you write reflects what you have to do in the assignment by comparing what you wrote to the instructor's assignment several times.

4. If possible, compare your retelling of the assignment to that of another classmate. If your work reveals different understandings of the assignment, look up words and concepts together. If you both still have a different understanding, ask your instructor to clarify the assignment.

How to Write a Compare and Contrast Essay

Comparison and contrast essays usually analyze the similarities and differences between two subjects. You might write an impartial paper that portrays both subjects, or you might show why you favor one over the other. Don't think you must choose an earth-shattering topic to write a good paper. On the contrary, you will do a better job if you are familiar or interested in the two subjects you choose.

What makes a compare and contrast essay unique? Think about what you have learned in class as well as your textbook reading before you complete the next activities.

Below is a list of steps that will help you gather ideas and draft your essay.

1. Generate ideas.

Activity: Pick subjects you can compare and contrast purposefully. You may choose two people, two events, two places, two objects, two activities, or two ideas, but be sure to choose two you care about. You'll need to choose things that have a sensible basis for comparison, a common element that makes it reasonable to compare and contrast the two. Besides having a common element, the subjects should share enough to compare but differ enough to contrast. If you are working with classmates, decide on a general category for comparison and contrast (music, films, local restaurants, smartphones, etc.) and spend five minutes calling out everything that you can think of that fits the category.

2. Pick a topic to compare.

Activity: When you finish brainstorming, select two subjects from the list of ideas you have jotted down. Freewrite for two minutes about the characteristics those subjects have in common, then for two more minutes about ways that they differ. Can you jot down several characteristics for each? When you are done pick the most workable pair.

3. Identify your purpose and audience.

Activity: Do you want to inform, persuade, or entertain your readers? Do you want to evaluate which of the objects is better? Which topics will your readers be most interested in? Picture your audience. What do you need to tell them? What do you want them to feel or understand when they read your essay?

4. Gather supporting evidence.

Activity: Find details and examples that will support your points. You can do this by interviewing someone at each event you're contrasting, or read news or other accounts. You can browse websites that supply different examples or look up articles reporting studies or government statistics. Identify facts and information that reinforce the ability of your readers to understand the subjects you are comparing and contrasting. What details will be most helpful in clarifying similarities and differences?

5. Develop a preliminary thesis statement.

Activity: What assertion do you want to make about the topic? In a comparison and contrast essay, the thesis should make a point so readers will understand why you are making this comparison and what you are concluding about it.

- Comparing _____ and _____ reveals important differences that matter because _____
  _____.

- _____ [one subject being compared] is beneficial for _____ [audience] because _____
  _____.

Reread the ideas you've come up with about your topic, and try writing a thesis statement of your own.

_____
_____
_____

6. Compare and contrast your subjects and organize your notes.

Activity: A comparison and contrast essay is usually organized in one of two ways: either point by point or subject by subject. A point-by-point organization (alternating pattern) addresses one aspect of one subject being discussed, then a related aspect of the other subject; another aspect of the first subject, then a related aspect of the second; and so on. A subject-by-subject (opposing pattern) comparison and contrast essay covers all aspects of the first subject being discussed before covering all the aspects of the second subject. Pick the strategy that you want to follow.

Point-by-point organization

➤ The first point of comparison for subject A _____

➤ The first point of comparison for subject B _____

➤ The second point of comparison for subject A _____

➤ The second point of comparison for subject B _____

➤ The third point of comparison for subject A _____

➤ The third point of comparison for subject B _____

A subject-by-subject comparison and contrast essay covers all aspects of the first subject being discussed before covering all the aspects of the second subject.

Subject-by-subject organization

➤ The first point of comparison for subject A _____

➤ The second point of comparison for subject A _____

➤ The third point of comparison for subject A _____

➤ The first point of comparison for subject B _____

➤ The second point of comparison for subject B _____

➤ The third point of comparison for subject B _____

_____

7. Sketch an outline.

Activity: Fill in the information below to help you develop an outline for your comparison and contrast essay.

Topic sentence of first body paragraph: _____

_____

Details about the subject and the point of comparison:
- _____
- _____
- _____

Topic sentence of second body paragraph: _____

_____

Details about the subject and the point of comparison:
- _____
- _____
- _____

Topic sentence of third body paragraph: _____

_____

Details about the subject and the point of comparison:
- _____
- _____
- _____

Topic sentence of fourth body paragraph: _____

_____

Details about the subject and the point of comparison:
- _____
- _____
- _____

(Continue until you have outlined or sketched a plan for all your body paragraphs.)

8. Draft your essay.

Activity: What part of the draft are you most excited about writing or do you feel best prepared to begin? Start with that part. If you have an idea for a solid jumping-off place, you can begin with an introduction, but you don't need to write the draft in the order it will be read; just get started. Make sure your conclusion reinforces the idea that you have an important reason for comparing the two subjects and leave readers with a comment on the comparison.

7

Explaining Causes and Effects

Cause-and-effect essays give information to answer *how*, *why*, or *what* questions. Rather than simply presenting and explaining information, as in a report, in a cause-and-effect essay you are giving potential reasons for why something happened or what its results might be and suggesting ways to address or solve a problem. To this work effectively, you have to gather information to help you recognize and analyze causes and effects. You can start by considering these questions:

1. What is a *cause*? What is an *effect*? Can you think of an example of each?
2. What does it mean to interpret information? If you are not sure, look up the word "interpret" in the dictionary.
3. What do you need in order to write a cause-and-effect essay?

Pre-assignment Questions

Think about what you have learned about cause-and-effect essays from your instructor and your textbook. After responding to the questions that follow, ask your instructor, a tutor, or a peer to help you answer any questions you still have.

1. Have you written a cause-and-effect essay before? If so, what was it about? Did you enjoy the process? If you have never written a cause-and-effect essay before, talk about a verbal explanation you have given to someone.
2. How do you feel about writing this essay? Are you worried about the process? Excited? Explain why you feel the way you do. If you have concerns, consider discussing them with a peer or your instructor.
3. Being proactive means anticipating challenges so that they don't get in your way. How can you proactively address anything that might get in the way of you writing an awesome essay? For example, if you struggle with procrastination, you might create a schedule that makes time for every step of

your work. If you struggle with writing clear or varied sentences, you might do some practice exercises in the "Additional Tools for Practice" section of this workbook.

Understanding Your Assignment

Make sure you understand your assignment before you get started. If your instructor gave you a choice of assignments, first select which assignment you are interested in completing. Read your assignment carefully and answer the questions that follow.

1. Based on the assignment that you were given, what type of cause-and-effect essay are you being asked to write? Are you writing about a major current or historical event? Are you writing about a personal habit or experience? Are you analyzing something in the past or predicting what might happen in the future?

2. Write down any words or concepts that you do not understand from the assignment. Consult your textbook or talk with your instructor for clarification. Skip this question if all the words and concepts are clear to you.

3. In your own words, in a way that is most understandable to you, retell what your instructor is asking you to do. Put any special requirements, as broad as topic suggestions and as narrow as font-size requirements, in your assignment retelling. Make sure what you write reflects what you have to do in the assignment by comparing what you wrote to the instructor's assignment several times.

4. If possible, compare your retelling of the assignment to that of another classmate. If your work reveals different understandings of the assignment, look up words and concepts together. If you both still have a different understanding, ask your instructor to clarify the assignment.

How to Write a Cause-and-Effect Essay

A cause-and-effect essay speculates (and finds research to back up) potential reasons for a problem, experience, or phenomenon. These could be general problems or personal experiences. Using situations you're familiar with could even help you do a better job.

What makes a cause-and-effect essay unique? Think about what you have learned in class as well as your textbook reading before you complete the next activities.

Below is a list of steps that will help you gather ideas and draft your essay.

1. Generate ideas.

Activity A: There are some people who go about their business in the world accepting things as they are and others who want to know why things are the way they are. Some people fit somewhere in the middle. There is no wrong way to be, but it's helpful to know where you fit for writing this paper. Where do you fit in this spectrum? Why do you think you have this response to the world? Activity B below is for people who already have some questions about the world, and Activity C is for those of you who are stumped.

Activity B: If you are a person who has wondered why certain things are the way they are, you likely have many possible topics for a cause-and-effect paper. Think of a question you have and write it here. Then brainstorm possible reasons for that phenomenon. Why do humans have ridges in their ears? Why does a particular form of social media appeal to teens? Why did an election have surprising results? Select your favorite question. If you do not have any questions, move to Activity C without answering this question.

Activity C: Write a list of the last four things that have been frustrating to you. For example, are you angry about having to take writing or math classes in college? Did you have to wait in a long line yesterday to get something that should have taken five minutes? Do you always get sick in the winter? Did a friend do something annoying? Then next to each of your statements, add the question words how, why, or what, and you have possible topics for your paper.

Examples: Why do colleges and universities still require traditional math and writing classes? How do the lines at pharmacies get so long? Why do college students get sick during the winter? What if all friendships ended when someone did something annoying?

2. Choose a topic.

Activity: This assignment leaves you the option of writing from what you know, what you can find out, or a combination of the two. Write down a list of three or four possible ideas about your topic from what you have observed or experienced.

3. Gather sources of support.

Activity: After identifying the topic you would like to cover, it's time to find examples. Go on the Internet, a library database, or go to the library. Take notes on possible reasons from other sources, making sure to cite where the source came from.

4. Write a draft of your introduction.

Activity: Introduce your reader to your research question along with why you are interested in the question. You may want to include some basic information you found for your topic in this paragraph.

5. Outline your paper.

Activity: Make a list of the possible answers to your question starting with the least plausible (possible) and ending with the most plausible (possible). Your paper can then follow this structure.

6. Draft your paper.

Activity: Since a cause-and-effect essay is, by nature, speculative, you will need to use a lot of qualifiers like *sometimes*, *perhaps*, and *possibly*. Practice writing at least three sentences for your paper that have these words in them before you complete your draft.

7. Integrate your evidence.

Activity: When integrating your evidence, tables, charts, and graphs can often consolidate information that illustrates causes or effects. Place any graphics near the related text discussion, supporting but not duplicating it. Aside from visual evidence, you can quote experts and include statistics that help support you topic. Be sure to cite your sources according to the documentation style your instructor has assigned.

8

Taking a Stand

When you take a stand on an issue you care about, you try to convince others to adopt your point of view. In person, taking a stand might mean protesting or debating. In writing, taking a stand means arguing for your position. When writing an argument, make sure that there are at least some others who feel differently from you. The point of an argument is to help people think in new ways about topics and even create solutions to issues in the world. Such writing is common in newspaper editorials, letters to the editor, or opinion columns in print and digital news outlets. It is also the foundation of persuasive essays, brochures, and blog posts.

Writing of this kind has a twofold purpose — to express your opinion and to win your readers' respect for it. Sometimes writers of arguments may also want to persuade their readers to take action. In order to write a strong argument you should establish your audience (who you are talking to) and who might disagree with you. You should also make sure that you offer evidence in the form of data, quotations, paraphrases, or summaries from other sources. When writing an argument, you can employ the strategy of pathos (appealing to readers' emotions), logos (appealing to logic), and ethos (establishing your character and credibility as an author) to engage readers' intellect, emotions, and sense of fairness and reason. You can start by considering these questions:

1. Is it a good idea to write an argument paper for an audience that feels the same way as you? Explain.
2. What is meant by *audience*?
3. What are some strategies you can use to engage your audience?

Pre-assignment Questions

Think about what you have learned about arguments from your instructor and your textbook. After responding to the questions that follow, ask your instructor, a tutor, or a peer to help you answer any questions you still have.

1. Have you written an argumentative essay before? If so, what was it about? Did you enjoy the process? If you have never written an argumentative essay before, you can write about a verbal argument you have had.

2. How do you feel about writing this essay? Are you worried about the process? Excited? Explain why you feel the way you do. If you have concerns, consider discussing them with a peer or your instructor.

3. Being proactive means anticipating challenges so that they don't get in your way. How can you proactively address anything that might get in the way of you writing an awesome argumentative essay? For example, if you struggle with procrastination, you might make a schedule that makes time for every step of your work. If you struggle with writing clear or varied sentences, you might do some practice exercises in the "Additional Tools for Practice" section of this workbook.

Understanding Your Assignment

Make sure you understand your assignment before you get started. If your instructor gave you a choice of assignments, first select which assignment you are interested in completing. Read your assignment carefully and answer the questions that follow.

1. Based on the assignment you were given, what type of argument are you being asked to write? An essay? A letter to an editor? Is it a proposal for or against a specific policy? A blog entry?

2. Write down any words or concepts that you do not understand from the assignment. Consult your textbook or talk with your instructor for clarification. Skip this question if all the words and concepts are clear to you.

3. In your own words, in a way that is most understandable to you, retell what your instructor is asking you to do. Put any special requirements, as broad as topic suggestions and as narrow as font-size requirements, in your assignment retelling. Make sure what you write reflects what you have to do in the assignment by comparing what you wrote to the instructor's assignment several times.

4. If possible, compare your retelling of the assignment to that of another classmate. If your work reveals different understandings of the assignment, look up words and concepts together. If you both still have a different understanding, ask your instructor to clarify the assignment.

How to Write an Argumentative Essay

An argumentative essay makes a claim that is supported by evidence. Your whole essay is directly linked to your opinion or stance. Your purpose isn't to solve a social or moral problem but to make clear exactly where you stand on an issue and to persuade your readers to respect your position, perhaps even accept it or act on it.

What makes an argumentative essay unique? Think about what you learned in class as well as your textbook reading before you complete the next activities.

Below is a list of steps that will help you gather ideas and draft your essay.

1. Generate ideas.

Activity: Write down a list of four issues or controversies that interest you. They might be current issues, long-standing ones, or matters of personal concern.

2. Choose a topic and take a stand.

Activity: Using the list above, write for five minutes about your listed topics. When you are done, look over the notes that you have made and decide which topic you will address. Write down where you stand on the issue, why your topic interests you, and any personal experiences you have had that relate to your topic.

3. Develop a thesis statement.

Activity: Turn your topic into a potential thesis statement by writing a claim about it. Your claim is your opinion.

Example: Boston should have more bilingual programs in elementary schools so that young immigrants can acclimate better and so that there can be more diversity in schools.

4. Write down supporting details.

Activity: Write down at least four details to support your claim. They may be as broad or focused as you like.

5. Determine the assumption behind your claim.

Activity: To be the most sensitive writer possible to your audience, think about the assumption that is underneath your claim. Consider the claim "Boston should have more bilingual programs in elementary schools so that young immigrants can acclimate better and so that there can be more diversity in schools." The assumption is that diversity in schools is valuable. Some audiences may not agree with this, so you would need to try to get your audience on board with your assumption as well as with your claim. Write your assumption or assumptions here.

6. Address counterarguments for your claim.

Activity: Write why people may not agree with you so that you can incorporate this into your essay and get those people on board. Some people like to write the counterargument in their first paragraph before their thesis statement to bring the other side in right away, and others like to wait to talk about counterarguments in individual paragraphs. For now, list at least three reasons why someone may not agree with your thesis.

7. Gather sources of support.

Activity: Now that you've stated your claim, you'll need evidence to support it. That evidence can be anything that demonstrates the soundness of your position and the points you make. Using a library database (Issues and Controversies, Academic Source Complete, LexisNexus, JSTOR), find at least four examples, statistics, or quotes from articles that support your point, and write at least three here.

8. Activate *pathos, logos,* and *ethos.*

Activity: Write down at least two examples to support your point that would appeal to your readers' emotions; two examples that would engage readers' intellect; and two examples that would draw on your readers' sense of fairness. A persuasive argument usually operates on all three levels.

9. Outline your paper.

Activity: Some instructors will give you a structure for writing your essay, and others will want that structure to come entirely from you. Make an outline using the information you have. Topic sentences usually contain a restatement of your claim and the example you are going to talk about in that paragraph. Using the information from the previous steps, write topic sentences for your body paragraphs and then write down which is the most convincing. Why do you think it will convince readers the most? This will help you decide on an order for your information when writing your outline.

Here is one structure for an outline:

> Introduction (introduce your subject and your thesis statement)
> Body Paragraph I (least convincing topic sentence and supporting evidence)
> Body Paragraph II (more convincing topic sentence and supporting evidence)
> Body Paragraph III (most convincing topic sentence and supporting evidence)
> Conclusions (summary of argument with memorable final thoughts)

10. Draft your essay.

Activity: Staying close to your outline, think of your readers as you draft, and appeal to them using logic, emotion, and ethics. Back yourself up with facts and be sure to credit your sources as you write.

How to Write a Counterargument

A refutation argument looks at the thesis/claims of another writer and takes an opposing stand.

What makes a refutation argument unique? Think about what you learned in class as well as your textbook reading before you complete the next activities.

Below is a list of steps that will help you gather ideas and draft your essay.

1. Find a source (perhaps from this semester or a previous semester) whose claim you did not agree with.

Activity: Write about one or more possible texts whose ideas you did not agree with. Reread at least one of these texts and write why you didn't agree with it. Make sure that you note the title of the article and the author's name.

2. Take a stand in response to the claim.

Activity: Write down the main claim you are refuting. This is the thesis of the author you do not agree with. You can state it directly in quotation marks or in your own words. The claim of an article is often partially contained in the title of the article. Sometimes it is in the first paragraph or conclusion paragraph.

3. Write down the author's main points.

Activity: Write down the main points that the author makes to support his or her claim. You may find these directly stated in paragraphs or you may have to look at individual paragraphs and come up with a general statement for what all of the details have in common.

4. Quote or paraphrase from the source article.

Activity: Quote or paraphrase at least three statements from the source article that you would like to make sure to refute in your paper.

5. Assess the opposing viewpoint.

Activity: Use these questions to help you assess your evidence from your standpoint: What is the writer's evidence? What are the strengths of the other position? What are the limitations? What facts, statistics, testimony, observation, or other evidence can you use to show why their claims are weak, only partially true, or misguided?

6. Gather supporting evidence.

Activity: You'll need evidence to support your counterargument. That evidence can be anything that demonstrates the soundness of your position and the points you make. Using a library database (Issues and Controversies, Academic Source Complete, LexisNexus, JSTOR), find at least four examples, statistics, or numbers that support your point, and write at least three here.

7. Make an outline.

Activity: Using the outline below as a model (if you need a model), make an outline for your refutation argument. Please note that a sub-claim here means anything that falls under a source author's claim. It can be a supporting detail or another small claim under the umbrella of his or her larger claim.

> Introduction (clear statement of source author's idea along with a thesis that states the reasons why you feel the author's claim is flawed)
>
> Body Paragraph I (restatement of author's sub-claim I and why this claim is flawed)
>
> Body Paragraph II (restatement of author's sub-claim II and why this claim is flawed)
>
> Body Paragraph III (restatement of author's sub-claim III and why this claim is flawed)
>
> Conclusions (clear and compelling new way to think of the problem or direct statement of your claim about the topic, as well as any final positive implications [positive consequences] of thinking of the author's idea differently).

8. Draft your essay.

Activity: Staying close to your outline, think of your readers as you draft, and appeal to them using logic, emotion, and ethics. Back yourself up with facts, and be sure to credit your sources as you write.

9

Proposing a Solution

You can use the power of your writing to solve a problem, to make something better, or to implement change. A proposal provides your readers with one or more solutions to a problem. It can also provide ideas for how to handle a situation or suggestions for the allocation of funds. The idea behind a proposal is transformation. You can start by considering these questions:

1. What is a proposal?
2. What does the word *allocate* mean? What type of proposal might involve suggestions for the allocation of funds?

Pre-assignment Questions

Think about what you have learned about proposal essays from your instructor and your textbook. After responding to the questions that follow, ask your instructor, a tutor, or a peer to help you answer any questions you still have.

1. Have you ever written a proposal before? If so, what was it about? Did you enjoy the process? If you have never written a proposal before, you can write about a verbal proposal you made to someone. Maybe you proposed to a friend that you get Hawaiian shave ice on the first day of spring. What did you say in the proposal? How did it turn out?

2. How do you feel about writing this essay? Are you worried about the process? Excited? Explain why you feel the way you do. If you have concerns, consider discussing them with a peer or your instructor.

3. Being proactive means anticipating challenges so that they don't get in your way. How can you proactively address anything that might get in the way of you writing an awesome proposal? For example, if you struggle with procrastination, you might create a schedule that makes time for every step of your work. If you struggle with writing clear or varied sentences, you might do some practice exercises in the "Additional Tools for Practice" section of this workbook.

Understanding Your Assignment

Make sure you understand your assignment before you get started. If your instructor gave you a choice of assignments, first select which assignment you are interested in completing. Read your assignment carefully and answer the questions that follow.

1. Based on the assignment you were given, what type of proposal are you being asked to write? Is it about a problem you care about and strongly wish to resolve? Is it large or small? Does it affect the whole country or mainly people from your city, campus, or classroom?

2. Write down any words or concepts that you do not understand from the assignment. Consult your textbook or talk with your instructor for clarification. Skip this question if all the words and concepts are clear to you.

3. In your own words, in a way that is most understandable to you, retell what your instructor is asking you to do. Put any special requirements, as broad as topic suggestions and as narrow as font-size requirements, in your assignment retelling. Make sure what you write reflects what you have to do in the assignment by comparing what you wrote to the instructor's assignment several times.

4. If possible, compare your retelling of the assignment to that of another classmate. If your work reveals different understandings of the assignment, look up words and concepts together. If you both still have a different understanding, ask your instructor to clarify the assignment.

How to Write a Proposal

In making a proposal, you urge action by using words like *should*, *ought*, and *must*. We propose solutions to problems all the time, both formally and informally.

What makes a proposal unique? Think about what you have learned in class as well as your textbook reading before you complete the next activities.

Below is a list of steps that will help you gather ideas and draft your essay.

1. Generate ideas.

Activity: Brainstorm by writing down all the problems that come to mind; jot down everything that frustrates you or could be changed in your world (school, family, community, etc.) Observe events around you, look in the news, browse websites or blogs, listen to the radio or podcasts.

2. Choose a topic.

Activity: From the ideas you generated above, choose a problem to focus on — a problem that you *want* to solve.

3. Determine your audience.

Activity: For proposals, you want to be aware of your audience. Write down who your main readers will be (your classmates, the college administration, elected officials, etc.). Also determine the audience of people who are in a position to change the situation. Usually these are people with money and/or power. Write down this audience as well. How will you draw in your audience? Your audience needs to believe that your problem is real and your solution is feasible. Look for ways to make it personal, to show that it affects them and deserves their attention.

4. Zoom in on a topic.

Activity: Write a paragraph describing the problem you want to write about. Think about the problem from all perspectives. Who is affected by it? Would government officials or academic administration have more information about it? What are the reasons behind the current situation?

5. List solutions to the problem.

Activity: Make a list of solutions to the issue (what you think should be done) and what would be needed for the solution to be achieved. Start with the most radical and least plausible (possible) option and move to the most reasonable. When writing these solutions, please keep in mind your target audience and the audience of those with money and/or power. Appeal to both audiences with your solutions.

6. List possible objections.

Activity: Make a list of possible objections your audience might raise—concerns about the cost, complexity, or workability of your plan, or new problems your solutions might cause. Persuade readers by anticipating and laying to rest their likely objections.

7. Gather sources of support.

Activity: To show that the problem really exists, you'll need evidence and examples. Find data about the problem, potentially from reputable media like the *New York Times*, the *Economist*, the *Wall Street Journal*, or your preferred local news source. Consider whether local history archives, accounts of public meetings, interviews, or relevant websites might help you develop your solution.

8. Make an outline.

Activity: Make an outline for your essay. Sometimes the author will start with a description of the problem and then states possible solutions. You decide how the information you wrote and gathered above should best be organized.

9. Draft your essay.

Activity: Staying close to your outline, think of your audience as you draft. Back yourself up with facts and specific detail, and be sure to credit your sources as you write.

10. Revise based on feedback.

Activity: Are people outraged? Are they on board? Revise your proposal based on the thoughts and feelings that your audience expresses.

10

Evaluating and Reviewing

Evaluating means judging. An evaluation provides your comments and assessments about anything in the world including ideas, people, products, and media. You do it when you decide what candidate to vote for, pick which smartphone to buy, or recommend a new restaurant to your friends. But to write an evaluation calls for you to think more critically. To create a convincing evaluation, you should have criteria for that evaluation, and then come up with evidence to back up your judgment. As with many forms of writing, good evidence is crucial in convincing people of your points. The subject might be a film, a book, or a performance that you review. Or it might be a sports team, a product, or a body of research that you evaluate. The possibilities are endless. You can start by considering these questions:

1. What is an evaluation?
2. What is meant by having criteria for an evaluation?
3. Explain why it is a good idea to have evidence in an evaluation essay.

Pre-assignment Questions

Think about what you have learned about evaluation essays from your instructor and your textbook. After responding to the questions that follow, ask your instructor, a tutor, or a peer to help you answer any questions you still have.

1. Have you written an evaluation or review before? If so, what was it about? Did you enjoy the process? If you have never written an evaluation or review before, you can write about a verbal evaluation or review you have given.
2. How do you feel about writing this essay? Are you worried about the process? Excited? Explain why you feel the way you do. If you have concerns, consider discussing them with a peer or your instructor.

3. Being proactive means anticipating challenges so that they don't get in your way. How can you proactively address anything that might get in the way of you writing an awesome essay? For example, if you struggle with procrastination, you might create a schedule that makes time for every step of your work. If you struggle with writing clear or varied sentences, you might do some practice exercises in the "Additional Tools for Practice" section of this workbook.

Understanding Your Assignment

Make sure you understand your assignment before you get started. If your instructor gave you a choice of assignments, first select which assignment you are interested in completing. Read your assignment carefully and answer the questions that follow.

1. Based on the assignment that you were given, what type of evaluation or review are you being asked to write? It can be an evaluation of a movie, a TV show, a work of art, a new product or service, a novel or poem, or anything else.

2. Write down any words or concepts that you do not understand from the assignment. Consult your textbook or talk with your instructor for clarification. Skip this question if all the words and concepts are clear to you.

3. In your own words, in a way that is most understandable to you, retell what your instructor is asking you to do. Put any special requirements, as broad as topic suggestions and as narrow as font-size requirements, in your assignment retelling. Make sure what you write reflects what you have to do in the assignment by comparing what you wrote to the instructor's assignment several times.

4. If possible, compare your retelling of the assignment to that of another classmate. If your work reveals different understandings of the assignment, look up words and concepts together. If you both still have a different understanding, ask your instructor to clarify the assignment.

How to Write an Evaluation

An evaluation takes stock of subject (person, idea, program, or phenomenon) and evaluates it. With specific criteria, your purpose is twofold: (1) to set forth your assessment of the quality of your subject and (2) to convince your readers that your judgment is reasonable.

What makes an evaluation unique? Think about what you have learned in class as well as your textbook reading before you complete the next activities.

Below is a list of steps that will help you gather ideas and draft your essay.

1. Generate ideas.

Activity: Write a list of possible topics to assess. You could write about how a popular musician is not really the best like many people think. You could assess the progress of a sports team or a particular presidential policy. Try *brainstorming* or *mapping* to identify as many possible topics as you can. Ask yourself which topics interest you most—and which will be the most interesting to evaluate or review. Test your understanding of each possible topic by describing or summarizing it.

2. Choose a topic to evaluate or review.

Activity: Look over the notes that you made on the previous step and select your topic.

3. Identify your criteria.

Activity: Write down how you are measuring what is good and what is not. These are called your criteria, or standards for evaluation, and they help your readers understand how you have made your judgment. Criteria focus on particular features of your subject, not just whether you like it or not. Put a star next to any criteria that your audience may not agree with.

4. Gather supporting evidence.

Activity: You'll want to spend time finding material to help you develop a judgment, such as facts, statistics, photos and illustrations, or firsthand observations. Write down three pieces of evidence to support your claim. Make sure that your evidence links to your criteria for evaluation so that readers know how and why you reach your judgment.

5. Make an outline.

Activity: Most writers find that an outline—even a rough list—helps them keep track of points to make. Will it be more effective to begin with your thesis and support it with evidence, or present your evidence first and end with your overall judgment? Following the format below or one like it, make an outline for your critical assessment essay.

>Introduction states what you are assessing: (subject and the overall criterion for assessment)
>
>Body Paragraph I: (subject and how it can be measured based on first criterion)
>
>Body Paragraph II: (subject and how it can be measured based on second criterion)
>
>Body Paragraph III: (subject and how it can be measured based on third criterion)
>
>Conclusion: (leaves the reader with an important point to think about or tells them what is at stake if topic is assessed differently)

6. Draft your essay.

Activity: Staying close to your outline, think of your audience as you draft. Back yourself up with facts and specific detail. Conclude by appealing to your readers to accept your evaluation or review.

Supporting a Position with Sources

Unlike a debate, an essay that takes a position generally doesn't have two sides or a single winner. Instead, the writer typically joins the ongoing exchange of ideas about an intriguing topic in the field. Writers conduct research — finding articles, essays, reports, and books that convey perspectives, research findings, and conclusions about the topic — to bolster their ideas. Having sources that support your position makes it stronger, as the facts, data, statistics, expert testimony, or other evidence can help convince your readers. You can start by considering these questions:

1. What is the difference between a debate and an essay that takes a position?
2. What is the purpose of using sources for this kind of essay?

Pre-assignment Questions

Think about what you have learned about supporting a position with sources from your instructor and your textbook. After responding to the questions that follow, ask your instructor, a tutor, or a peer to help you answer any questions you still have.

1. Have you ever written an essay that uses source material to support a position before? If so, what was it about? Did you enjoy the process? If you have never written an essay based on sources before, you can write about a time when you had a conversation in which you were explaining your position on a specific matter and used evidence (a news story, a photograph, a quotation from someone involved in the situation) to support your ideas.
2. How do you feel about writing this essay? Are you worried about the process? Excited? Explain why you feel the way you do. If you have concerns, consider discussing them with a peer or your instructor.

3. Being proactive means anticipating challenges so that they don't get in your way. How can you proactively address anything that might get in the way of you writing an awesome essay? For example, if you struggle with procrastination, you might create a schedule that makes time for every step of your work. If you struggle with writing clear or varied sentences, you might do some practice exercises in the "Additional Tools for Practice" section of this workbook.

Understanding Your Assignment

Make sure you understand your assignment before you get started. If your instructor gave you a choice of assignments, first select which assignment you are interested in completing. Read your assignment carefully and answer the questions that follow.

1. Based on the assignment you were given, what type of source-based essay are you being asked to write? Are you writing an essay based on a topic your professor assigned or are you brainstorming your own topic? What type of sources should you draw upon to support your position?

2. Write down any words or concepts that you do not understand from the assignment. Consult your textbook or talk with your instructor for clarification. Skip this question if all the words and concepts are clear to you.

3. In your own words, in a way that is most understandable to you, retell what your instructor is asking you to do. Put any special requirements, as broad as topic suggestions and as narrow as font-size requirements, in your assignment retelling. Make sure what you write reflects what you have to do in the assignment by comparing what you wrote to the instructor's assignment several times.

4. If possible, compare your retelling of the assignment to that of another classmate. If your work reveals different understandings of the assignment, look up words and concepts together. If you both still have a different understanding, ask your instructor to clarify the assignment.

How to Write an Essay that Supports a Position with Sources

A source-based essay takes a position and supports it with information from research sources. It considers what readers will ask about the issue and provides evidence to convince them that the position taken is the correct one.

What makes a source-based essay that takes a position unique? Think about what you learned in class as well as your textbook reading before you complete the next activities.

Below is a list of steps that will help you gather ideas and draft your essay and support it with sources.

1. Read to generate ideas.

Activity: Perhaps your instructor has assigned the topic and required readings to use as sources. Try to develop curiosity about the subject. Look for an angle that will engage you, or consider how the topic might relate to your own experience. If the topic and sources were not assigned, identify a cluster of readings about a topic that interests you. Draw on your experiences, interests, conversations, and imagination, and think of topics that you are eager to learn more about. Take notes, jotting down a list of potential topics.

2. State your position.

Activity: Look over the notes that you have made on the previous question and choose a topic to address. Read more about the topic you choose to write about and write down questions raised by your reading. Based on the information you've gathered from your reading, develop a position about the topic that you'd like to share with an audience of college readers.

3. Draft a thesis statement.

Activity: Turn your topic into a potential thesis statement by writing a claim about it. Your claim is your opinion.

Example: Even with good health insurance, dealing with the paperwork and red tape of getting coverage for your care during a health crisis contributes unnecessary stress and uncertainty to the situation. Health insurance companies should streamline their processes, accepting doctor recommendations for care rather than challenging their necessity.

4. Gather supporting evidence.

Activity: Support your position—your working thesis—using quotations, paraphrases, summaries, and syntheses of the information in the readings as evidence. Look for a variety of sources that will broaden and challenge your perspective. Go to an online database at the library (Issues and Controversies, JSTOR, Academic Source Complete, LexisNexus, or others), and make sure to present your information from sources clearly and credit your sources appropriately.

5. Sketch an outline.

Activity: Many instructors differ in their opinions about writing outlines. Some instructors will give you a structure for writing your essay, and others will want that structure to come entirely from you. Make an outline using the information you have, and talk with your instructor to find out more. Regardless of whether you or your instructor comes up with the structure of the essay, your outline should clearly state your position and should mention the kinds of evidence you will provide from sources.

6. Draft your essay.

Activity: Staying close to your outline, back yourself up with your sources, and craft a compelling introduction and a satisfying conclusion by appealing to your readers to accept your position.

7. Don't forget about your own voice.

Activity: Finding your own voice may be difficult in a source-based essay. By the time you have supported your position by quoting, paraphrasing, or summarizing relevant readings, you may worry that your sources have taken over your paper. Don't let them dominate your writing. To make sure your voice dominates your essay, reread your drafts and identify where the voices of others have become louder than yours.

Responding to Literature

A literary reflection or analysis gives you a chance to comment on an experience with literature, a specific book, or a larger cultural phenomenon related to literature. It requires you to read closely a literary work (short story, novel, play, or poem) and then to divide it into elements, explain its meaning, and support your interpretation with evidence from the work. The purpose of a literary reflection or analysis is to illuminate the meaning of the work, to help you and others understand it better. Doing literary reflections or analyses can help you even if you are not an English major because they encourage critical thinking, making you more sensitive to your inner realities and to your environment. You can start by considering these questions:

1. What is literature? What types of topics might you write about for a literary analysis?
2. What is meant by *phenomenon related to literature*?
3. Explain what the purpose of a literary analysis is.

Pre-assignment Questions

Think about what you have learned about literary reflection or analysis from your instructor and your textbook. After responding to the questions that follow, ask your instructor, a tutor, or a peer to help you answer any questions you still have.

1. Have you written a literary reflection or an analysis before? If so, what was it about? Did you enjoy the process? If you have never written one, write down a book that you have read and enjoyed. If you have never read a full book, write down the title of a book you wish you had read or plan to read (maybe for this assignment).

2. How do you feel about writing this essay? Are you worried about the process? Excited? Explain why you feel the way you do. If you have concerns, consider discussing them with a peer or your instructor.

3. Being proactive means anticipating challenges so that they don't get in your way. How can you proactively address anything that might get in the way of you writing an awesome literary reflection or analysis? For example, if you struggle with procrastination, you might create a schedule that makes time for every step of your work. If you struggle with writing clear or varied sentences, you might do some practice exercises in the "Additional Tools for Practice" section of this workbook.

Understanding Your Assignment

Make sure you understand your assignment before you get started. If your instructor gave you a choice of assignments, first select which assignment you are interested in completing. Read your assignment carefully and answer the questions that follow.

1. Based on the assignment that you were given, what type of literary reflection or analysis are you being asked to write? Is it a comparison and contrast of two literary works or a critical analysis of a single work? Have you been assigned a specific literary text, or can you choose one?

2. Write down any words or concepts that you do not understand from the assignment. Consult your textbook or talk with your instructor for clarification. Skip this question if all the words and concepts are clear to you.

3. In your own words, in a way that is most understandable to you, retell what your instructor is asking you to do. Put any special requirements, as broad as topic suggestions and as narrow as font-size requirements, in your assignment retelling. Make sure what you write reflects what you have to do in the assignment by comparing what you wrote to the instructor's assignment several times.

4. If possible, compare your retelling of the assignment to that of another classmate. If your work reveals different understandings of the assignment, look up the words and concepts together. If you both still have a different understanding, ask your instructor to clarify the assignment.

How to Write about Literature

A literary analysis looks at a particular piece of literature. It can look at a small part of the literary work, or it can look at a piece of literature more broadly. In either case, it makes a claim about the literature.

What makes a literary analysis unique? Think about what you have learned in class as well as your textbook reading before you complete the next activities.

Below is a list of steps that will help you gather ideas and draft your essay.

1. Choose a type of close reading.

Activity: Below is a list of various types of close readings. Please highlight the type that you would like to do.

- Looking at two texts closely, make a claim about two literary readings.
- Analyze plot, character, setting, theme, language, symbol, or image in one text.
- Interpret a text. In other words, talk about how the literary elements come together to form a particular meaning that you want to put forth.
- Talk about the context of the text. This is a paper about the author of the text or the culture at the time it was written; it uses specific parts of the text to support your points. You might also talk about how an author's influences are clear in the text.

2. Decide on your texts.

Activity: This will, in part, be determined by your instructor's assignment instructions, but take a moment to write about a book or books you might be interested in. Your selection might be a short story, poem, a play, a novel, or a graphic novel. Do not worry about how this comes out. Just write your thoughts, feelings, and ideas about what you might like to write about. Then write a little bit about how you might do the type of close reading that you selected above.

3. Brainstorm to identify elements.

Activity: First, make sure you understand the literal meaning (exactly what is happening) of the text you chose, and then consider its figurative meaning (the symbolic or metaphorical meaning). Consult a glossary of literary terms for ideas.

4. Draft a thesis.

Activity: Make a tentative thesis about the book or books you will be writing about. Try and focus on one element (such as character, setting, or theme) or the interrelationship of two or three elements (such as characterization and symbolism). For example: "The text of *Extremely Loud and Incredibly Close*, by Jonathan Safron Foer, prepares the reader for its blank pages." This could be a paper about how the language in the novel *Extremely Loud and Incredibly Close* anticipates a few blank pages in the book, and you would explain how various other passages in the book get us ready for the experimental blank pages. Along the way you might find something better to write about, but it's good to see what you can find as a first step.

5. Look for examples in the text.

Activity: Read your texts over again and look for examples to prove your thesis. Write them down. These examples can provide you with quotations to use as evidence in your essay.

6. Come up with topic sentences.

Activity: If you are happy with your information, create topic sentences to organize your examples. These will become the topic sentences for your paragraphs.

7. Make use of the Internet.

Activity: Most college students do not have the time to read a text twelve times to see exactly where an author used the word blue (especially if the text is over 100 pages). If you're looking for a particular word or phrase in a book, go to an online resource like Project Gutenberg that offers the full text of books for free online. Then do a page search (often by pressing command-F or control-F, on the computer keyboard) to look for a particular word or phrase. You will still need to find that phrase in your book, but noting that it's in chapter 3 using a web source can save you a lot of time. Make a list here of examples you think you still need or parts you can't find. You may also be able to ask a classmate to help you fill in these gaps.

8. Make an outline.

Activity: Sketch out an outline of your essay, beginning with your working thesis. Organize your essay around specific points that support your interpretation. Support each point you make with evidence from the text.

9. Draft your essay.

Activity: Staying close to your outline, back yourself up with specific references to the text. Be sure to cite each reference as your instructor has specified.

Responding to Visual Representations

Visual representations are everywhere, and they affect how we think of ourselves and the world around us. They can take countless familiar forms, including magazine covers, cereal boxes, graffiti, television advertisements, or slideshow presentations. They can be made up of many pieces, including still images, moving images, spoken words, written words, music, color, and ambient noise. When a visual representation catches our eye, we have the opportunity to think about how it communicates a message, what the intended message might be, what group or groups of people the message is for, and whether the visual representation succeeds in reaching those people. Most of us are used to letting visual representations wash over us. Because there are so many all around us, the idea of picking one apart might be intimidating. You can start by considering these questions:

1. Why do you think people sometimes use visual representations to convey ideas?
2. What does it mean to respond to or analyze something? If you are unsure, look up "analyze" in a dictionary and use your textbook's index to find discussions and examples of analysis.

Pre-assignment Questions

Think about what you have learned about visual representations from your instructor and your textbook. After responding to the questions that follow, ask your instructor, a tutor, or a peer to help you answer any questions you still have.

1. Have you written about a visual representation before? If so, what kind of visual representation was it? A photograph or advertisement, for example? Did you enjoy thinking and writing about it? If you have never written about a visual representation, think about an image that has caught your eye at some point. What was the image, and what were your thoughts about it?

2. How do you feel about responding to a visual representation? Are you worried about the process? Excited? Explain why you feel the way you do. If you have concerns, consider discussing them with a peer or your instructor.

3. Being proactive means anticipating challenges so that they don't get in your way. How can you proactively address anything that might get in the way of successfully writing about a visual representation? For example, if you struggle with procrastination, you might create a schedule that makes time for every step of your work. If you struggle with writing clear or varied sentences, you might do some practice exercises in the "Additional Tools for Practice" section of this workbook.

Understanding Your Assignment

Make sure you understand your assignment before you get started. If your instructor gave you a choice of assignments, first select which assignment you are interested in completing. Read your assignment carefully and answer the questions that follow.

1. Based on the assignment, what type of visual representation will you write about? Some examples include photographs, paintings, billboards, public service announcements, print advertisements, and commercials.

2. Write down any words or concepts that you do not understand from the assignment. Consult your textbook or talk with your instructor for clarification. Skip this question if all the words and concepts are clear to you.

3. In your own words, in a way that is most understandable to you, retell what your instructor is asking you to do. Put any special requirements, as broad as topic suggestions and as narrow as font-size requirements, in your assignment retelling. Make sure what you write reflects what you have to do in the assignment by comparing what you wrote to the instructor's assignment several times.

4. If possible, compare your retelling of the assignment to that of another classmate. If your work reveals different understandings of the assignment, look up words and concepts together. If you both still have a different understanding, ask your instructor to clarify the assignment.

How to Write about Visual Representation

A visual representation conveys meaning through feeling or mood, attitude, language, signs or symbols, and overall theme.

What makes a visual representation an effective mode of communication? Think about what you have learned in class as well as from your textbook reading before you complete the next activities.

Below is a list of steps that will help you gather ideas and draft your essay.

1. Select a visual representation to analyze.

Activity: If your instructor has not assigned a specific visual representation for analysis, select one on your own. Look for visuals that catch your eye and promise rich detail for analysis. What kind of visual representation is it? A photograph or an advertisement?

2. Describe your visual.

Activity: Just as you annotate a written text, do the same to record your observations of the image you chose. In other words, describe what happens in it. What do you see? What people, objects, or animals are pictured? What colors appear? Write down any written or spoken words that are included. If there is sound, what do you hear?

3. Describe how you feel when viewing your subject.

Activity: How does the visual representation make you feel? Hopeful or fearful? Sad, happy, angry? Why do you think you feel that way? Do you think others are likely to feel the same way when viewing the visual representation you have chosen? Why or why not?

4. Research your visual and its origins.

Activity: Find out who created your visual and when and where it was first published or exhibited. What company or organization created it? What is its purpose? What is the story behind the final product?

5. Consider the audience.

Activity: Who do you think is the intended audience of the visual representation? How can you tell? And how does the visual representation appeal to that audience? If an image of a lonely puppy appears, you might assume that the creator of the visual intended to reach animal lovers. If a lonely teenager appears, the intended audience might be other teenagers who feel alone as well as anyone who might be encouraged to recognize signs of loneliness in the teens around them. Who or what appears in the visual representation and how do the pictured people, animals, places, or things relate to the audience?

6. Dig into the details.

Activity: Now that you have recognized all of the features of your visual representation and gathered some background information, consider the details. What elements are emphasized by placement, size, or color. What is most prominent? Something that appears in the foreground or in bright color or large type is usually important. If there are words, how would you describe the font? Playful or serious? Is anything in all capital letters? Is anything blurry or sharply focused? If there is sound, is it loud or quiet, fast or slow? How do these details make you feel?

7. Draft a thesis about the visual representation.

Activity: What is the purpose of the visual representation? In other words, what does the creator intend to convey to the audience? Combine the information you gathered in steps 2 through 6 to determine your interpretation of the image, and identify details that support your thesis. Your thesis may also address whether or not the visual succeeds in connecting with its intended audience.

8. Write a draft of your introduction.

Activity: Introduce your reader to the visual representation you are writing about. You may want to include some basic information about your subject to help orient your readers. Include your thesis statement, so that readers understand what you intend to say and why it matters.

9. Outline your paper.

Activity: Now that you have decided what you want your readers to understand about the visual representation you have chosen, think about what information you need to share with them so that they fully understand your position and find it reasonable. Your notes about the background and details of the visual representation will come in very handy here. Think of a way to organize your thoughts so that your reader can follow them. For example, if the visual representation includes images, written words, and sounds, you might plan to devote a body paragraph to each of these elements.

10. Draft your paper.

Activity: Using your outline as a guide, draft paragraphs to flesh out your ideas about the visual representation, and support those ideas with your research and observations. Make sure you discuss the plot and theme of the visual representation. Your draft should be clear and detailed enough that even readers who have never thought about this particular visual representation before will understand your ideas and find them reasonable. End with a conclusion that reinforces your interpretation.

PART THREE

Additional Tools for Practice

- **14** Sentence Guides for Academic Writers   71
- **15** Writing Grammatically Correct Sentences   80
- **16** Writing Clear Sentences in a Thoughtful Style   86
- **17** Activities for Improving Your Writing   98

Sentence Guides for Academic Writers

Being a college student means being a college writer. No matter what field you are studying, your instructors will ask you to make sense of what you are learning through writing. When you work on writing assignments in college, you are, in most cases, being asked to write for an academic audience.

Writing academically means thinking academically—asking a lot of questions, digging into the ideas of others, and entering into scholarly debates and academic conversations. As a college writer, you will be asked to read different kinds of texts; understand and evaluate authors' ideas, arguments, and methods; and contribute your own ideas. In this way, you present yourself as a participant in an academic conversation.

What does it mean to be part of an *academic conversation*? Well, think of it this way: You and your friends may have an ongoing debate about the best film trilogy of all time. During your conversations with one another, you analyze the details of the films, introduce points you want your friends to consider, listen to their ideas, and perhaps cite what the critics have said about a particular trilogy. This kind of conversation is not unlike what happens among scholars in academic writing—except they could be debating the best public policy for a social problem or the most promising new theory in treating disease.

If you are uncertain about what academic writing *sounds like* or if you're not sure you're any good at it, this chapter offers guidance for you at the sentence level. It helps answer questions such as these:

> How can I present the ideas of others in a way that demonstrates my understanding of the debate?
>
> How can I agree with someone, but add a new idea?
>
> How can I disagree with a scholar without seeming, well, rude?
>
> How can I make clear in my writing which ideas are mine and which ideas are someone else's?

The following sections offer sentence guides for you to use and adapt to your own writing situations. As in all writing that you do, you will have to think about your purpose (reason for writing) and your audience (readers) before knowing which guides will be most appropriate for a particular piece of writing or for a certain part of your essay.

The guides are organized to help you present background information, the views and claims of others, and your own views and claims — all in the context of your purpose and audience.

Academic Writers Present Information and Others' Views

When you write in academic situations, you may be asked to spend some time giving background information for or setting a context for your main idea or argument. This often requires you to present or summarize what is known or what has already been said in relation to the question you are asking in your writing.

Presenting What Is Known or Assumed

When you write, you will find that you occasionally need to present something that is known, such as a specific fact or a statistic. The following structures are useful when you are providing background information.

- As we know from history, _____.
- X has shown that _____.
- Research by X and Y suggests that _____.
- According to X, _____ percent of _____ are/favor _____.

In other situations, you may have the need to present information that is assumed or that is conventional wisdom.

- People often believe that _____.
- Conventional wisdom leads us to believe _____.
- Many Americans share the idea that _____.
- _____ is a widely held belief.

In order to challenge an assumption or a widely held belief, you have to acknowledge it first. Doing so lets your readers believe that you are placing your ideas in an appropriate context.

- Although many people are led to believe X, there is a significant benefit to considering the merits of Y.
- College students tend to believe that _____ when, in fact, the opposite is much more _____.

Presenting Others' Views

As a writer, you build your own *ethos*, or credibility, by being able to fairly and accurately represent the views of others. As an academic writer, you will be expected to demonstrate your understanding of a text by summarizing the views or arguments of its author(s). To do so, you will use language such as the following.

- X argues that _____.
- X emphasizes the need for _____.
- In this important article, X and Y claim _____.
- X endorses _____ because _____.
- X and Y have recently criticized the idea that _____.
- _____, according to X, is the most critical cause of _____.

Although you will create your own variations of these sentences as you draft and revise, the guides can be useful tools for thinking through how best to present another writer's claim or finding clearly and concisely.

Presenting Direct Quotations

When the exact words of a source are important for accuracy, authority, emphasis, or flavor, you will want to use a direct quotation. Ordinarily, you will present direct quotations with language of your own that suggests how you are using the source.

- X characterizes the problem this way: "...."
- According to X, _____ is defined as "...."
- "...," explains X.
- X argues strongly in favor of the policy, pointing out that "...."

Note: You will generally cite direct quotations according to the documentation style your readers expect. MLA style, often used in English and in other humanities courses, recommends using the author name paired with a page number, if there is one. APA style, used in most social sciences, uses the past tense (*concluded, argued*) and requires the year of publication generally after the mention of the source, with page numbers after the quoted material. In *Chicago* style, used in history and in some humanities courses, writers use superscript numbers (like this[6]) to refer readers to footnotes or endnotes. In-text citations, like the ones shown below, refer readers to entries in the works cited or reference list.

MLA	Lazarín argues that our overreliance on testing in K-12 schools "does not put students first" (20).
APA	Lazarín (2014) argued that our overreliance on testing in K-12 schools "does not put students first." (p. 20)
Chicago	Lazarín argues that our overreliance on testing in K-12 schools "does not put students first."[6]

Many writers use direct quotations to advance an argument of their own:

Student writer's idea

Source's idea

> Standardized testing makes it easier for administrators to measure student performance, but it may not be the best way to measure it. Too much testing wears students out and communicates the idea that recall is the most important skill we want them to develop. Even education policy advisor Melissa Lazarín argues that our overreliance on testing in K–12 schools "does not put students first" (20).

Presenting Alternative Views

Most debates, whether they are scholarly or popular, are complex — often with more than two sides to an issue. Sometimes you will have to synthesize the views of multiple participants in the debate before you introduce your own ideas.

- On the one hand, X reports that _____, but on the other hand, Y insists that _____.
- Even though X endorses the policy, Y refers to it as " . . . ."
- X, however, isn't convinced and instead argues _____.
- X and Y have supported the theory in the past, but new research by Z suggests that _____.

Academic Writers Present Their Own Views

When you write for an academic audience, you will indeed have to demonstrate that you are familiar with the views of others who are asking the same kinds of questions as you are. Much writing that is done for academic purposes asks you to put your arguments in the context of existing arguments — in a way asking you to connect the known to the new.

When you are asked to write a summary or an informative text, your own views and arguments are generally not called for. However, much of the writing you will be assigned to do in college asks you to take a persuasive stance and present a reasoned argument — at times in response to a single text and at other times in response to multiple texts.

Presenting Your Own Views: Agreement and Extension

Sometimes you agree with the author of a source.

- X's argument is convincing because _____.
- Because X's approach is so _____, it is the best way to _____.
- X makes an important point when she says _____.

Other times you find you agree with the author of a source, but you want to extend the point or go a bit deeper in your own investigation. In a way, you acknowledge the source for getting you so far in the conversation, but then you move the conversation along with a related comment or finding.

- X's proposal for _____ is indeed worth considering. Going one step further, _____.
- X makes the claim that _____. By extension, isn't it also true, then, that _____?
- _____ has been adequately explained by X. Now, let's move beyond that idea and ask whether _____.

Presenting Your Own Views: Queries and Skepticism

You may be intimidated when you're asked to talk back to a source, especially if the source is a well-known scholar or expert or even just a frequent voice in a particular debate. College-level writing asks you to be skeptical, however, and approach academic questions with the mind of an investigator. It is acceptable to doubt, to question, to challenge — as the result is often new knowledge or understanding about a subject.

- Couldn't it also be argued that _____?
- But is everyone willing to agree that this is the case?
- While X insists that _____ is so, he is perhaps asking the wrong question to begin with.
- The claims that X and Y have made, while intelligent and well-meaning, leave many unconvinced because they have failed to consider _____.

Presenting Your Own Views: Disagreement or Correction

You may find that at times the only response you have to a text or to an author is complete disagreement.

- X's claims about _____ are completely misguided.
- X presents a long metaphor comparing _____ to _____; in the end, the comparison is unconvincing because _____.

It can be tempting to disregard a source completely if you detect a piece of information that strikes you as false or that you know to be untrue.

- Although X reports that _____, recent studies indicate that is not the case.

It can be tempting to disregard a source completely if you detect a piece of information that strikes you as false or that you know to be untrue.

- Although X reports that _____, recent studies indicate that is not the case.
- While X and Y insist that _____ is so, an examination of their figures shows that they have made an important miscalculation.

> **A NOTE ABOUT USING THE FIRST PERSON ("I")**
>
> Some disciplines look favorably upon the use of the first person "I" in academic writing. Others do not and instead stick to using the third person. If you are given a writing assignment for a class, you are better off asking your instructor what he or she prefers or reading through any samples given than *guessing* what might be expected.
>
> **First person (I, me, my, we, us, our)**
>
> > I question Heddinger's methods and small sample size.
> >
> > Harnessing children's technology obsession in the classroom is, I believe, the key to improving learning.
> >
> > Lanza's interpretation focuses on circle imagery as symbolic of the family; my analysis leads me in a different direction entirely.
> >
> > We would, in fact, benefit from looser laws about farming on our personal property.
>
> **Third person (names and other nouns)**
>
> > Heddinger's methods and small sample size are questionable.
> >
> > Harnessing children's technology obsession in the classroom is the key to improving learning.
> >
> > Lanza's interpretation focuses on circle imagery as symbolic of the family; other readers' analyses may point in a different direction entirely.
> >
> > Many Americans would, in fact, benefit from looser laws about farming on personal property.
>
> You may feel that not being able to use "I" in an essay in which you present your ideas about a topic is unfair or will lead to weaker statements. Know that you can make a strong argument even if you write in the third person.

Presenting and Countering Objections to Your Argument

Effective college writers know that their arguments are stronger when they can anticipate objections that others might make.

- Some will object to this proposal on the grounds that _____.
- Not everyone will embrace _____; they may argue instead that _____.

Countering, or responding to, opposing voices fairly and respectfully strengthens your writing and your *ethos*, or credibility.

- X and Y might contend that this interpretation is faulty; however, _____.
- Most _____ believe that there is too much risk in this approach. But what they have failed to take into consideration is _____.

Academic Writers Persuade by Putting It All Together

Readers of academic writing often want to know what's at stake in a particular debate or text. They want to know why it is that they should care and that they should keep reading. Aside from crafting individual sentences, you must, of course, keep the bigger picture in mind as you attempt to persuade, inform, evaluate, or review.

Presenting Stakeholders

When you write, you may be doing so as a member of a group affected by the research conversation you have entered. For example, you may be among the thousands of students in your state whose level of debt may change as a result of new laws about financing a college education. In this case, you are a *stakeholder* in the matter. In other words, you have an interest in the matter as a person who could be impacted by the outcome of a decision. On the other hand, you may be writing as an investigator of a topic that interests you but that you aren't directly connected with. You may be persuading your audience on behalf of a group of interested stakeholders—a group of which you yourself are not a member.

You can give your writing some teeth if you make it clear who is being affected by the discussion of the issue and the decisions that have been or will be made about the issue. The groups of stakeholders are highlighted in the following sentences.

- Viewers of Kurosawa's films may not agree with X that _____.
- The research will come as a surprise to parents of children with Type 1 diabetes.
- X's claims have the power to offend potentially every low-wage earner in the state.
- Marathoners might want to reconsider their training regimen if stories such as those told by X and Y are validated by the medical community.

Presenting the "So What"

For readers to be motivated to read your writing, they have to feel as if you're addressing something that matters to them, addressing something that matters very much to you, or addressing something that should matter to us all. Good academic writing often hooks readers with a sense of urgency—a serious response to a reader's "So what?"

- Having a frank discussion about _____ now will put us in a far better position to deal with _____ in the future. If we are unwilling or unable to do so, we risk _____.
- Such a breakthrough will affect _____ in three significant ways.
- It is easy to believe that the stakes aren't high enough to be alarming; in fact, _____ will be affected by _____.

- Widespread disapproval of and censorship of such fiction/films/art will mean _____ for us in the future. Culture should represent _____.
- _____ could bring about unprecedented opportunities to participate in _____, something never seen before.
- New experimentation in _____ could allow scientists to investigate _____ in ways they couldn't have imagined _____ years ago.

Presenting the Players and Positions in a Debate

Some disciplines ask writers to compose a review of the literature as a part of a larger project or sometimes as a free-standing assignment. In a review of the literature, the writer sets forth a research question, summarizes the key sources that have addressed the question, puts the current research in the context of other voices in the research conversation, and identifies any gaps in the research.

Writing that presents a debate, its players, and their positions can often be lengthy. What follows, however, can give you the sense of the flow of ideas and turns in such a piece of writing.

Student writer states the problem.

_____ affects more than 30 percent of children in America, and signs point to a worsening situation in years to come because of A, B, and C. Solutions to the problem have eluded even the sharpest policy minds and brightest researchers.

Student writer summarizes the views of others on the topic.

In an important 2003 study, W found that _____, which pointed to more problems than solutions. [. . .] Research by X and Y made strides in our understanding of _____ but still didn't offer specific strategies for children and families struggling to _____. [. . .] When Z rejected both the methods and the findings of X and Y, arguing that _____, policymakers and health care experts were optimistic. [. . .]

Student writer presents her view in the context of current research.

Too much discussion of _____, however, and too little discussion of _____, may lead us to solutions that are ultimately too expensive to sustain.

Using Appropriate Signal Verbs

Verbs matter Using a variety of verbs in your sentences can add strength and clarity as you present others' views and your own views.

WHEN YOU WANT TO PRESENT A VIEW FAIRLY NEUTRALLY

acknowledges	observes
adds	points out
admits	reports
comments	suggests
contends	writes
notes	

- X points out that the plan had unintended outcomes.

WHEN YOU WANT TO PRESENT A STRONGER VIEW

    argues   emphasizes
    asserts   insists
    declares

- Y argues in favor of a ban on _____; but Z insists the plan is misguided.

WHEN YOU WANT TO SHOW AGREEMENT

    agree
    confirms
    endorses

- An endorsement of X's position is smart for a number of reasons.

WHEN YOU WANT TO SHOW CONTRAST OR DISAGREEMENT

    compares   refutes
    denies   rejects
    disputes

- The town must come together and reject X's claims that _____ is in the best interest of the citizens.

WHEN YOU WANT TO ANTICIPATE AN OBJECTION

    admits
    acknowledges
    concedes

- Y admits that closer study of _____, with a much larger sample size, is necessary for _____.

15

Writing Grammatically Correct Sentences

Correcting Sentence Boundary Issues

Sometimes we need to set personal boundaries in life. Have you ever been in a particularly clingy relationship where a friend or a person you are dating only wants to spend time with you and maybe even acts like you are one and the same person? Depending on your personality and needs, you might have brought the issue to the person's attention and said that you needed space to be your own person. This means you set a personal boundary. Sentences need boundaries too. They need to be complete on their own, and they need appropriate space from other sentences to communicate their full meaning.

What is often tricky about sentence boundaries is that they are based on grammatical rules and not on whatever you might think is logical. If you haven't spent a lot of time reading books, articles, and other print materials and observing how sentences function in them, you will need to learn how sentences function grammatically to understand their boundaries and how to write them with confidence. Do not despair! In the age of social media, there is mass confusion about what makes up a complete sentence, and I would argue that the rules will eventually change to meet our evolving needs. For now, here are some activities to help you learn how to set sentence boundaries correctly.

Activities

Take a look at the sentences below and circle which is correct:

1. I often go to parties with my friends, my friends are more social than I am.
2. I often go to parties with my friends; my friends are more social than I am.
3. I often go to parties with my friends, but my friends are more social than I am.

The final sentence might be the best option, but both of the last two sentences are grammatically correct. Some students think that the first is correct because the topic stays the same throughout the sentence. You are writing about friends and parties the whole time, so that should be a complete sentence, right? In other languages, such as Japanese, sentences are arranged by topic, but this is not true in English. The first sentence is a type of run-on sentence called a comma splice. It is missing the appropriate punctuation, instead splicing together two complete thoughts with only a comma. These two complete thoughts need better boundaries than what a comma provides.

To have a complete sentence, you need to have at least one complete thought, at least one verb, and at least one subject. Grammatically speaking, a "complete thought" is what we call an **independent clause**. It's independent because, much like an independent person with good boundaries, it is complete and can stand alone. "I often go to parties with my friends" is an independent clause because it has a subject ("I"), a verb ("go"), and is a complete thought that can stand alone as its own complete sentence. Likewise, "My friends are more social than I am" is also an independent clause because it has a subject ("My friends"), a verb ("are"), and is a complete thought that can stand alone as its own complete sentence as well.

If you have two separate independent clauses, such as in this example, and they are fused together (meaning, no punctuation divides them) or spliced together with a comma (as in example 1), they form a **run-on sentence**, which means they have poor boundaries and are grammatically incorrect.

To put two or more independent clauses into a single complete sentence requires the use of either a **conjunction** (such as *and, but, for, or,* or *so*) preceded by a comma (example 3) or a stronger linking punctuation mark than a comma (such as a colon or a semicolon, as in example 2). When two independent clauses are properly joined, as in examples 2 and 3 above, they unite to form a complete sentence.

Relatedly, if you have a grouping of words that forms an incomplete thought, is missing a verb, or is missing a subject, you have a **sentence fragment**. For example, "Parties with my friends," is a sentence fragment. Most obviously, it is missing a verb and is not a complete thought. It raises too many questions. It cannot stand alone as an independent clause, and it cannot stand alone as a complete sentence. Let's define these terms simply.

A **subject** is what is being or doing the verb. ("*I* often go. . . .")

A **verb** is a state of being experienced by the subject or action done by the subject. ("I often *go*. . . .")

An **independent clause** is a complete thought that contains, at the very least, a subject and a verb. It can stand alone as a complete sentence.

A **run-on sentence** joins two independent clauses incorrectly, causing sentence boundary confusion.

A **conjunction** is a linking word, such as *and, but,* or *or,* that can be used to join two clauses.

A **dependent clause** has a subject and a verb, but it is an incomplete thought and therefore cannot stand alone. Consider the independent clause, "I often go to parties with my friends." If it had a word like *while* at its start, it would become dependent on more information to make it complete: "While I often go to parties with my friends." That clause no longer stands alone; it is dependent.

A **sentence fragment** is when a dependent clause or any other kind of incomplete thought is incorrectly treated as if it were complete. A sentence fragment is never a complete sentence.

Another term you need to know is **prepositional phrase**, since prepositional phrases can get in the way of you identifying subjects and verbs. A prepositional phrase contains a preposition that often shows where something is or when it is.

Identifying Subjects and Verbs

Circle the subjects and underline the verbs in the sentences below and write why you selected your answers:

1. In life we often set personal boundaries.
2. Sentences have boundaries too.
3. Some students think that the first sentence is correct because the topic stays the same throughout the sentence.
4. The first sentence is a run-on sentence.
5. It is missing the appropriate punctuation.
6. The verb is sometimes the action in the sentence.
7. I want to get better at correcting errors.
8. I love grammar.
9. On Tuesdays, I go to the learning lab.
10. I left my paper on my bed.

The Implied You

One common area of confusion that students often struggle with relates to the "implied you."

Often when there is a command, the subject, you, is implied rather than explicitly written down.

For example, one might say, "Sit down." This is a complete sentence because the "you" being spoken to is clearly implied and therefore, for all intents and purposes, present in the sentence.

Look at the "implied you" sentences below and identify the verb.

1. Sit down.
2. Stand up.
3. Go for a walk.
4. Know that I love you.
5. Sing loudly.

Correcting Sentence Fragments

Now that you know what a complete thought, verb, and subject are, you can correct the sentence fragments below. Remember that the minimum one needs for a complete sentence is a subject (clearly implied or explicitly stated), a verb, and a complete thought. These sentence fragments lack a complete thought, a subject, a verb, or a combination of these.

Correct each sentence fragment below. Explain why you corrected it as you did.

1. The minimum one needs.
2. Now that you know.
3. Correcting sentence fragments.
4. Susan.
5. Which is why it's important to proofread your papers.
6. The reason why I struggle with grammar.
7. Because I often procrastinate.
8. Into the paper.

Your Sentences

Write down ten sentences from a recent paper you wrote. Identify the subjects, verbs, and complete thoughts in your sentences. Next, note if any of the sentences are run-ons or fragments. It's fine if they are perfectly correct sentences! This is just an opportunity to look at your sentences in isolation from the rest of your paper. Why do you think it might be a good idea to look at your sentences in isolation from the rest of your paper?

Run-Ons and Fragments in Context

Look at the paragraph below, and highlight all run-ons and fragments. Then rewrite the paragraph correctly.

> Kimberly, a student at Community College of Philadelphia, was brilliant. But she wasn't very good at identifying run-ons and fragments. It seemed to her that her sentences were fine because they made sense when she read the whole paper, no one really taught her grammar rules either. Which made her really frustrated. One day Kimberly went to the learning lab and learned the rules for correcting sentences. And fragments. She was overjoyed. On her next paper, she still had a lot of run-on and fragment errors but not as many. Be like Kimberly! When you struggle with your writing, don't be afraid to ask for help. Even if you usually don't need it.

Run-Ons and Fragments in the Real World

Go outside your classroom, dorm room, office, or wherever you are right now, and look at the kinds of sentences you see on signs, buildings, fliers, and the like. Note three run-on sentences you find in the world. Then note three sentence fragments. Now write each incorrect run-on sentence and sentence fragment. Beneath each, please correct the sentence so that it is a complete sentence with appropriate boundaries. Sometimes these errors are intentional, as in a paper that says *For Sale* as a title, and sometimes they are not intentional, as in *Call me, I have a great Math 116 textbook for only $60.*

Pronouns

Pronouns like *I, you, he, she, it, we, they, this,* or *that,* are wonderful because they mean we do not have to keep saying the noun over and over and over again. Pronouns help us avoid situations like this:

Students often have to stand in line at financial aid. Students may not want to do this because they have to attend to their studies. Students sometimes do not have a choice.

In these sentences, using the word *they* for students would help create some variety.

Sometimes, if there are multiple nouns in a sentence or the opposite — no clear noun that the pronoun is referring to, you can confuse your reader.

Look at the examples below, then complete the activity.

Students often have to go to the financial aid window where the financial aid officers are in charge of answering questions. They can get frustrated.

The pronoun that is challenging here is *they*. Does *they* refer to the financial aid officers or the students? It may be that both are true, but as a writer you have to make clear what you mean. Here are two options for correcting the sentence above.

Students often have to go to the financial aid window where the financial aid officers are in charge of answering questions. Students can get frustrated.

or

Students often have to go to the financial aid window where the financial aid officers are in charge of answering questions. Both students and financial aid officers can get frustrated.

Another problem that often arises in papers is the nebulous (unclear) use of *this* or *that*. Imagine that you have just discussed various philosophers' points about ethics. You end your paragraph with:

This shows that there is no precise definition for ethics.

Do you mean the varying ideas of all the philosophers you spoke about in the paragraph? The ideas of the last philosopher you talked about? Your ideas? In this instance, you need to substitute *this* for a clear noun or group of nouns so your reader knows what you are referring to.

Look at the sentences below. Circle or highlight the confusing pronoun or pronouns and then rewrite the sentence with a more specific noun or nouns.

EXAMPLE:

➤ Original sentence: Reports give your readers information about various topics. They may or may not be familiar to your reader.

Rewritten sentence: <u>Reports give your readers information about various topics. The topics may or may not be familiar to your reader.</u>

1. There are different types of love according to the ancient philosophers. This is true today.
2. Revisions are important because they help you to communicate your ideas. They can often be unclear at first.
3. Lin-Manuel Miranda wrote *Hamilton* after reading a book about Alexander Hamilton. To many, he is considered a genius.
4. Oftentimes, people think of gender as something fixed at birth, but it really is a social construct. That is the problem.
5. Professors could do a better job meeting the evolving needs of students. They often forget how emotionally overwhelming college can be.
6. Dan doesn't really like his pet turtle. He makes a lot of noise at night.
7. Students often want to do well, but they don't know the steps to take for writing essays. These can be daunting.
8. You might focus your binoculars on a whale in the distance or you may be interested in pointing your binoculars toward a boat party to spy on it! It is different in each of these instances.
9. It may feel helpful when someone tells you the answers to grammar questions or math problems, but they don't always stick unless you learn how to find them on your own.
10. They often write essays in the first person. It is a good strategy for writing narrative essays, but they sometimes have a hard time transitioning to more objective writing for reports.

Pronouns in Your Work

Find an essay or short piece of writing that you have completed. Write down two consecutive sentences that have pronouns in them or one sentence that has a noun followed by another sentence with a pronoun. Identify the nouns/pronouns and explain why your pronoun references are clear or whether you should revise them. Please note that you do not need to find sentences with errors for this activity. The act of identifying pronouns in two consecutive sentences in your work will help to prime your brain to check for pronoun references the next time you write.

Writing Clear Sentences in a Thoughtful Style

Sentence Combination

The way sentences are constructed dictates how readers engage with our work. More complex sentences challenge readers' minds. Shorter sentences can give them a break to process information. Sentences constructed entirely in the same way can be overwhelming to your readers and might make them put down your essay. Therefore, it's good to practice the skill of sentence combination so that you are able to create sentence variety in your papers.

Look at the same example from the pronoun section on page 84:

Students often have to go to the financial aid window where the financial aid officers are in charge of answering questions. Students can get frustrated.

These two sentences can be combined into a smoother sentence in a variety of ways. Here are some options:

Students often have to go to the financial aid window where the financial aid officers are in charge of answering questions, and students can get frustrated.

This option simply uses the conjunction *and* to add information to the sentence. It emphasizes the word *students* by repeating it. The sentence gives the reader a sense that students are the most important preoccupation of the reader and perhaps subtly implies the severity of the financial aid officers' impact on students.

Students can get frustrated when they have to go to the financial aid window where financial aid officers are supposed to answer their questions.

This option places the frustration first and shifts the sentence slightly to be about how the officers are supposed to answer questions but likely don't. The emphasis in this sentence is less on the students and more on the challenges that the financial aid officers pose to students.

Financial aid workers, the people in charge of answering student questions, can often frustrate students.

This option puts financial aid workers job title as the subject and focuses mainly on how their actions frustrate students.

The distinctions are very subtle, but as a writer, you have complete control over how you want your thoughts to be perceived. All of these options are valid, and they will add texture to your paper. They will also help you to shape your emphasis at any given moment. Think about the various methods for sentence combination and complete the activity below.

Activity

Write down what you believe is the most effective combination of each pair of sentences below.

1. The student wanted to do a good job. He was only a freshman and didn't have the same skills as his peers.
2. Sometimes, the scholars disagree on definitions of terms. The way you define something can change your perception of it.
3. Lin-Manuel Miranda liked hip-hop as a child. Lin-Manuel Miranda's father was a political consultant.
4. A research report is an objective essay that presents information on a topic that you have investigated. It is not a personal essay.
5. An infographic is a report that includes visual elements. For example, you might include graphics of cigarettes if you are creating an infographic about smoking on campus.
6. Explanations give information to answer *how*, *why*, or *what* questions. They do not simply present information.
7. A causal analysis speculates potential reasons for a problem or phenomenon. A causal analysis also uses research to back up the speculations.
8. One point of an argument is to help people think in new ways about topics. Another point is to create solutions to issues in the world.
9. A proposal provides your readers with one or more solutions to a problem. It can also provide ideas for how to handle a situation or suggestions for the allocation of funds.
10. Below is a list of steps for creating an exploratory essay. Each activity is intended to get you thinking about what to do for each step.

Sentence Combination in Your Work

Activity

Write down three pairs of sentences from a recent essay you have written. Practice combining the sentences after you write down the originals.

Subject/Verb Agreement

In English, subjects and verbs have to agree in number. In other words, you should not have a singular subject like *he* paired with a plural verb like *know*. In order to understand this concept, please read the following and then complete the activity.

We have the following pronouns or words that stand in for nouns:

Singular (one)

I
You
He/ She /It

Plural (more than one)

We
You
They

Infinitives

An infinitive is the pure form of the verb. In English, an infinitive always has the word "to" before it. "To swim" is the infinitive and "I swim" is first person singular. The infinitive "to be" is not used in academic written English as a conjugation. Example: *You are happy* instead of *You be happy*.

Third Person Singular

In academic written English, remember to include an "s" in the third person singular construction.

EXAMPLES:

➤ She walks to the store.

➤ Mary knows the answer.

➤ There she goes.

Conjugations

If you are ever unsure of how to make a subject and verb agree, look up the following in a search engine: "English conjugation of the infinitive _____."

Example: "English conjugation of the infinitive to go." In addition to any verb conjugations you may have trouble with, please memorize the following:

To Be (present tense → happening now)

I am
You are
He/She/It is
We are
They are

To Be (past tense → happened then)

I was
You were
He/She/It was
We were
They were

To Have (present tense → happening now)

I have
You have
He/She/It has
We have
They have

To Have (past tense → happened then)

I had
You had
He/She/It had
We had
They had

To Go (present tense → happening now)

I go
You go
He/She/It goes
We go
They go

To Go (past tense → happened then)

I went

You went

He/She/It went

We went

They went

Activity

Now correct the subject/verb errors in the sentences below. All of the sentences should remain in the present tense. The present tense tells what is happening now.

1. She go to the store.
2. The dog walk every day.
3. They reads many books.
4. The weather be intense.
5. The student learn very easily.
6. We knows the answer.
7. The stars, in the sky, is visible.
8. The snowflake fall on my nose.
9. You asks too many questions.
10. One way to be happy are by reading.

Vocabulary Development in Papers

There are many ways to improve your vocabulary and the strategy that many college students choose is to look up synonyms (words that mean the same thing) in a thesaurus. The problem with this method is that, oftentimes, the words don't mean exactly the same thing. If you have never used the word before, you will be missing subtle denotations and connotations of the words In other words, the new potentially "bigger" word you choose will be communicating something different from what you'd like to communicate. First, answer the following questions about this paragraph and your vocabulary development process. Then, complete the activity.

1. What is *denotation*?
2. What is *connotation*?
3. When you want to increase your vocabulary in general, what do you personally do and why?
4. When you want to improve your vocabulary in your papers, what do you do and why?

Activity

One way to try out new words that works really well is using words you have seen or heard before. You are likely reading books or articles that have *new* words in them. By *new*, I do not necessarily mean words you've never *seen* before, but I do mean words you have never *used* before. Go back into one or more books or articles that you have read for this class and find some vocabulary words you personally have not used from these sources. List them below. After the word, write, in quotation marks, the sentence where it appeared in the book or article. Write the dictionary definition of the word that is closest to the meaning in the sentence where it appears. Then write your own sentence with the word.

Activity

Try to incorporate two of the words above into your next paper. To do that, write your topic and then brainstorm possible sentences that might contain the vocabulary word. For example, let's say the topic of your next paper is homelessness and one of your vocabulary words is *obfuscate*. You might write the following sample sentence:

Sometimes existing resources for homeless people obfuscate the problems that still exist for homeless populations.

Notice that the practice sentence contains the word "homeless," which is part of your theme. It also contains your vocabulary word. You don't need to force the exact sentences you write below into your paper, but it's helpful to think about possible sentences before you write the next paper. That way, your brain is primed to try to use a few new words.

Once you've completed the activity, ask yourself: Did this process work for you? If so, why? If not, what other techniques might you try?

Specificity and Precision of Language

Sometimes people feel that specificity and precision of language is reserved for personal and narrative essays or other forms of creative writing. You can certainly hone your precision skills through practicing these forms of writing, and in fact, the first activity below is going to ask you to do just that! However, specificity and precision of language is important for every type of essay you write. Even if you are writing a research report, the language you use and the specificity of your details can make a difference between an A paper and a C paper. It can make a difference in your reader understanding what you are saying or putting your paper down. The stakes can be higher than you think! The activities below are intended to help you develop precision in your language.

Has a teacher ever written "be specific" in the margins of your paper? If so, how did you react? Do you think you are good at using specific, precise words in your paper or is this something you need to work on? Explain why or why not.

Activity

The haiku is a form of creative writing that was invented in Japan. It is a poetic form that often has a prescribed set of syllables or voiced vowel sounds in each line. Haiku are short sensory glimpses into the world. One of the main reasons why writing a couple of haiku can help you with attention to language and precision is that they are very short. Unlike your papers that are pages long, many haiku follow the pattern of five syllables (line 1), seven syllables (line 2), and then five syllables (line three). Contemporary haiku do not always follow that exact pattern. Look at the sample haiku below by contemporary haiku poet Barry George, which has a different syllabic pattern but the same three lines and a more traditional second line. After reading Barry George's poems, complete the activities.

> after the storm
> he is rich in umbrellas —
> the homeless man
>
> off to school
> a father and two
> little umbrellas
>
> *Credit: Barry George*

1. What image or object appears in both poems? How does it appear differently in both poems?
2. Which of the five senses do these poems most appeal to? How do you know?

Activity

1. What is an object that is near you right now that is interesting to you or one about which you have a strong opinion? For example, does your mechanical pencil keep breaking? Is someone's bright red sweater still hanging on the hook in the back of the room? Write that object here.
2. Write one or more haiku about that object. Be as specific as possible.
3. Now take any three lines of a recent essay and turn them into a haiku using the traditional syllabic pattern.
4. Look at your haiku. What do you need to add to make it more interesting? What might you need to take away?
5. Revise your haiku.

Description and Paragraph Expansion

In order to describe objects, moments, or ideas, it is a good idea to use specific language. The activity below is designed to get you thinking about how to describe specifically and how to expand your paragraphs without just "padding" them for the sake of hitting page quotas.

To describe, think of the senses (touch, taste, smell, sight, hearing). Instead of saying *the bucket*, say *the blue bucket with the smooth handle that I found on my fourth birthday*.

To expand paragraphs, ask yourself who, what, where, when, why questions. For example, if you described a reason for a political policy, you might then talk about who was involved.

Activity

Select a photograph that speaks to you. Then write a paragraph that is as specific as possible that is about or inspired by that photograph.

Highlight two sentences that could be made more sensory and one sentence that could be expanded to answer *who, what, where, when, why, how* questions. Then rewrite the paragraph. Make sure it is more sensory and expanded.

Activity

Take a look at the sentences below and turn them into sentences that are more specific, following the example below.

Original Sentence: There are many homeless people in Philadelphia.

Revision A: Amid the hustle and bustle of shoppers on 17th and Walnut Street in Philadelphia, you will find corners speckled with homeless veterans asking for money.

Revision B: According to Project Home, there were 15,000 Philadelphians who used shelters in 2015 (Facts on Homelessness).

Note that the way you revise your sentences depends on the type of paper that you are writing. Sometimes you have to add precision through your language choices. As was true in your haiku, the first revision makes the sentence much more sensory and engaging. The second revision, appropriate for forms of writing like reports, explanations, and evaluations, adds specific information, in this case data about the use of shelters in Philadelphia.

1. **Original Sentence:** I walk home from school late at night.
2. **Original Sentence:** This college has a lot of extracurricular programs.
3. **Original Sentence:** In 2018 President Trump made a policy that impacted many people.
4. **Original Sentence:** The dollhouse was disturbing.
5. **Original Sentence:** The president of the college has more to do with student success or failure than you would think.
6. **Original Sentence:** *Wicked* is a good musical.
7. **Original Sentence:** The impact of the arts is widespread.
8. **Original Sentence:** The ladybug walked on my paper, and I had an idea.
9. **Original Sentence:** I learned to read because my mom made me.
10. **Original Sentence:** The best way to grow is to be open to changing your perspective.

Activity

Select a paper that you have written recently and write down at least five sentences that you might be able to revise. First write the type of paper it is and the conventions of that paper. In other words, can you revise your sentences using subjective information (opinion-based) or do you need to stick to the facts? Is there room for more creative and/or sensory sentences in this paper? After you have answered these questions, work on revising some of your sentences. Please note that you may want to steer away from the topic sentences (the first sentences of each paragraph) as they can often be intentionally general.

Transitions

Transitions help your reader get smoothly from one sentence to the other or one part of an essay to another. Sometimes you can use transition words to achieve this movement. Sometimes it is best to form a bridge between sentences instead of repeating the language in one sentence in the next sentence. If a park is missing bridges, the people who visit may fall into the water.

Activity

Draw a literal bridge between the two figures below.

Figure 1: Stick Drawing

Here are two sentences about the picture above. Circle the sentence pairing that contains the most helpful transition.

1. *There were two stick figures on the page. They were basically the same.*
2. *The two siblings were mostly the same. However, one had a hairstyle that made the other jealous.*

The second sentence contains a helpful transition. You might also form a bridge transition between the two sentences like this:

3. *The two siblings were basically the same. Their similarity ended with hairstyle.*

Note that the repetition of the *same/their similarity* helps to link the two sentences together.

Activity

Below is a list of selected transition words. Look at the list and then complete the activity by adding a transition word or creating a bridge transition between the two sentences.

To Add Information: In addition, Additionally, In the same way

To Show Contrast: However, In contrast, Even though

Examples: In other words, That is to say, For example

Space: In the center, To the left, To the right

Time: First, Second, Third, Later, Formerly

Now create a transition between each of the sentences below.

1. **Original Sentences:** Sometimes violence can be invisible. There are many women and men who suffer from emotional abuse.
2. **Original Sentences:** In our society, children sometimes can't get enough to eat. They can't get enough emotional support.
3. **Original Sentences:** Going to watch a dancing show can provide great emotional relief to you, especially if you are a busy college student. It's not the best idea on the night before a paper you haven't started is due.
4. **Original Sentences:** The first step to writing a successful essay is to decide you want to write it. Get out your computer.
5. **Original Sentences:** The photograph by Cindy Sherman contains a long-faced clown in the center of the composition. There are rainbow colors.
6. **Original Sentences:** There were two orange tabbies. They were basically the same.

Activity

Find pairs of sentences in a paper you have recently written. Create new transitions between each of the sentences. Please note that you may have perfectly excellent transitions between your sentences already, but experimenting with different transitions can really help you to practice different transition strategies that are available to you.

Research Skills

Paraphrasing

People tend to find paraphrasing challenging because it forces you to understand sentences on a very deep level. If you do not understand a sentence fully, you will not be able to paraphrase it accurately. Do not be intimidated! Paraphrasing can be mastered with practice.

Paraphrasing is putting a short amount of text in your own words while still giving proper credit to the author in the form of a citation. There are many ways to do this including looking at a sentence, looking away from the sentence, and magically putting it in your own words! Some people, especially those who have a lot of experience with reading and/or research, do not have to go through individual steps for this process. However, these steps can be very helpful if you are struggling with paraphrasing or if you want to get better at paraphrasing.

Paraphrasing Steps

1. Read the sentence(s) and understand it/them in the context of the article. Then write the sentence down with quotation marks.
2. Do a vocabulary annotation on the sentence (write down the vocabulary words and their definitions).
3. Put the sentence in your own words in your head or out loud to a friend.
4. Change the syntax (order) of your reworded sentence and make sure it still makes sense.
5. Your sentence should be about the same length as the original.
6. Create the citation (Author Page Number).

   EXAMPLE:

   ➤ *Quotation:* "Community College of Philadelphia should have better athletic equipment," according to Jeb Jones, a student at the college who wrote about the issue in an essay entitled "CCP Needs Work" (4).

   ➤ *Paraphrase:* According to Jeb Jones, in an essay called "CCP Needs Work," there could be much improvement in the paraphernalia for sports at the college (4).

What is different about the paraphrased example? Why is there a number four in parenthesis?

Activity

1. Select an article that you have read this semester and write down the title and the author.
2. Select a quotation from the article that is at least two consecutive sentences. After the quotation, write the page number following the model above. Then do a vocabulary annotation on the quotation.
3. Paraphrase, starting with the second sentence and moving to the first. Add a citation to your paraphrase.
4. Read your paraphrase. Does it make sense on its own? Does it mean the same as the original? If not, rewrite it, remembering to still include the citation.

Quotation Sandwich

Have you ever gone to a fast-food restaurant and been given a burger with a bun missing? Hopefully not! What would it be like if you went to a restaurant expecting a full burger and just being handed the meat from the center? First, it might get on your hands and make your hands sticky. It would be hard to eat and probably not taste so good. You would probably ask for your money back. When you are incorporating a quotation into an essay, you also want to make sure that you don't just provide your readers with the meat of your paragraph (the quotation). You have to give the readers something to hold onto to understand your quotation. Below is a method for incorporating quotations into paragraphs.

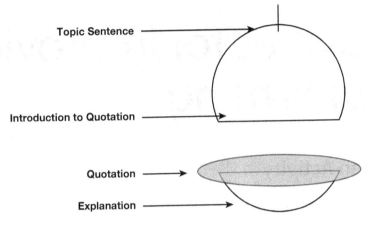

Figure 2: Burger Writing Image

Quotation: "Community College of Philadelphia should have better athletic equipment like badminton rackets that don't break and fully inflated basketballs" (Jones 4).

Paragraph Incorporating Quotation

One of the ways that Community College of Philadelphia could be improved is to improve various aspects of its athletic program. There are often articles written in the school newspaper about this topic. A recent article by Jeb Jones stated, "Community College of Philadelphia should have better athletic equipment like badminton rackets that don't break and fully inflated basketballs" (4). I agree with Jones that the school should purchase better athletic equipment. The other day, I went to the athletic center and a badminton racket broke while I was playing. One way that the school could get money for better equipment would be to have a raffle after graduation.

Activity

1. Highlight each of the hamburger labels in a different color and then highlight the sample paragraph with corresponding colors. For example, you could highlight the topic sentence next to the hamburger in pink and highlight the topic sentence of the paragraph in pink.
2. Write down a quotation with citation.
3. Practice putting that quotation in a quotation sandwich paragraph following the example above.

Activities for Improving Your Writing

Revision Activity

1. Write about the process of writing your last essay. What did you do first, second, third, etc.?
2. Write about any academic challenges you had writing your last essay.
3. Write about any emotional challenges you had writing your last essay (example: procrastination).
4. What do you want to make sure you do next time regarding your essay process?
5. What do you want to make sure you don't do next time regarding your essay process?
6. Based on your instructor's feedback, what are three specific skills you are going to work on before you write your next essay? For example: *I am going to reread my essay a third time to look for run-on sentences and sentence fragments. I will make sure that I add three more specific details than last time. I will write a longer conclusion.*

Peer Review Activity

First read your partner's essay. Then answer the following questions.

1. Review the possible structure for your partner's essay. Below, write down at least three sentences that follow the essay structure. Label these sentences with their names. Some examples include topic sentences, thesis statements, introduction, and so on.
2. Write down the most specific or precise moment in the essay and explain whether or not it is effective.

3. Write down a sentence where vocabulary is being used well in the essay.

4. If you feel comfortable, offer two specific critiques of your partner's writing. Please do not offer critiques in areas where you most struggle. For example, if you routinely make sentence boundary errors, focus instead in offering suggestions in essay structure (if you have had success in essay structure).

5. Discuss your answers with your partner. Then write down what you learned from reading your partner's essay.

Thesis Statement Activity

This activity can be done with fellow classmates inside or outside of the classroom. Follow the steps below to write a compelling and effective thesis statement.

1. On an index card or piece of paper, write down the thesis statement for whatever essay you are working on, following the guidelines you were given in class or the guidelines in your textbook.

2. Get at least four people to stand at the front of the room and read your thesis statement to them.

3. If they agree with your thesis statement they should move to the right and if they disagree with it they should move to the left. If they are confused or neutral, they should stand in the middle.

4. Ask the people at the front questions about why they are standing where they are standing and take notes.

If there are a lot of people in the middle, your thesis statement may not be arguable enough. Some people may be confused by your thesis statement and also be in the middle. If everyone is agreeing, consider your audience. Is your audience people who already agree with you? Do you want this? If everyone disagrees, make a note that you have to convince your audience. If the people in the front of the room give examples for their perspectives, write them down to potentially use (with attribution) or refute as needed. Feel free to switch roles after you have gotten the notes you need.

Topic Sentences Activity

Depending on the type of essay you are writing, the topic sentences can be very different. Here is an activity to help you with essays that are less analytical and contain more narrative elements.

Highlight the topic sentences and tell how you know that they are the topic sentences.

1. Here is an overview of a place that's significant to my life: Atlantic City. Atlantic City is in New Jersey. It takes two hours to get there. It has go-carts and an art cave. The beach is nice and relaxing. The water is very cold; it has shells in the water. Atlantic City is always crowded. The restaurants are good.

My family and I go there every summer. We always walk the boardwalk, which is very long. There are many opportunities to have fun with your family in Atlantic City!

2. My family and I have a lot of memories there. My mom gets free rooms so we always stay at the Four Seasons or Bally's hotel. One time when we were at Four Seasons, my brothers and I took a four-hour-long walk on the beach at 7 a.m. This was a great memory because usually we do not like each other, but this time we really bonded. In addition, I remember going to the all-you-can-eat buffet and trying crab legs for the first time when I was very young while in Atlantic City. I would like to continue to make memories there.

Using Models Activity

Follow the steps below to look deeply at a piece of writing that is the same as your piece of writing.

1. Write down the type of writing that you are working on here. For example, research study, argument, persuasive essay, etc.

2. Find an essay that is in the genre you are writing. Use your writing textbook to find the article or go online to your library database. You might have a sample from your teacher or even use a successful sample student essay provided by your teacher. Below is a selected list of websites that you can use to find articles in the genre that you may be writing if you do not have access to these sources. Note, find these sources by going into a search engine and typing in both the genre and the source (ex: feature story, *New York Times*). If the type of article you are writing is not listed below, type the genre with the word "example" into a search engine or ask your instructor or fellow classmate for ideas.

    a. Feature Story — *New York Times* or *The Guardian* online
    b. Research Report — *Rockefeller Archive Center*
    c. Infographic — *Wired*
    d. Causal Analysis — *Science Direct*
    e. Research Study — *Psychology Today*
    f. Flow Diagram — *Google Image*
    g. Argument — *Washington Post* Op Ed Section

3. Decide how you want to work with the article. The instructions below will ask you to highlight/copy down information, so if you have access to a printer or copy machine, that might be a good strategy. You might also write down the information for the following questions in your notebook or in a document on a computer.

4. What is the title of the piece? Does the title make clear the genre of the piece? What about the title might inspire a title for your piece or a revision of your current title?

5. Does this piece contain a thesis statement? If so, what is it and where is it located. Is the thesis statement direct or implied? Is the thesis statement or lack of thesis statement consistent with what you learned about this genre of writing?

6. Copy down or highlight the first sentence of the first three paragraphs in this essay (excluding the introductory paragraph). Do these sentences convey the overall point of the paragraphs or do they serve a different function? What can you learn from them?

7. Write down two supporting details in this essay. Do the supporting details tend to be personal examples, statistics, quotations from other sources? All of the above? Make a comment about how these points are balanced in the article. Are all personal examples in one paragraph and all statistics in another? Is there a blend of information?

8. Write down three vocabulary words in this piece of writing. How might you use them in your writing?

9. What is contained in the conclusion of this essay? How is it structured?

10. What do you find to be successful about the content of the article (the overall points the article is making)?

11. What do you find to be successful about the structure and rhetorical strategies of the article (how it was written)? What strategies would you like to use in your paper or in a revision of your paper.

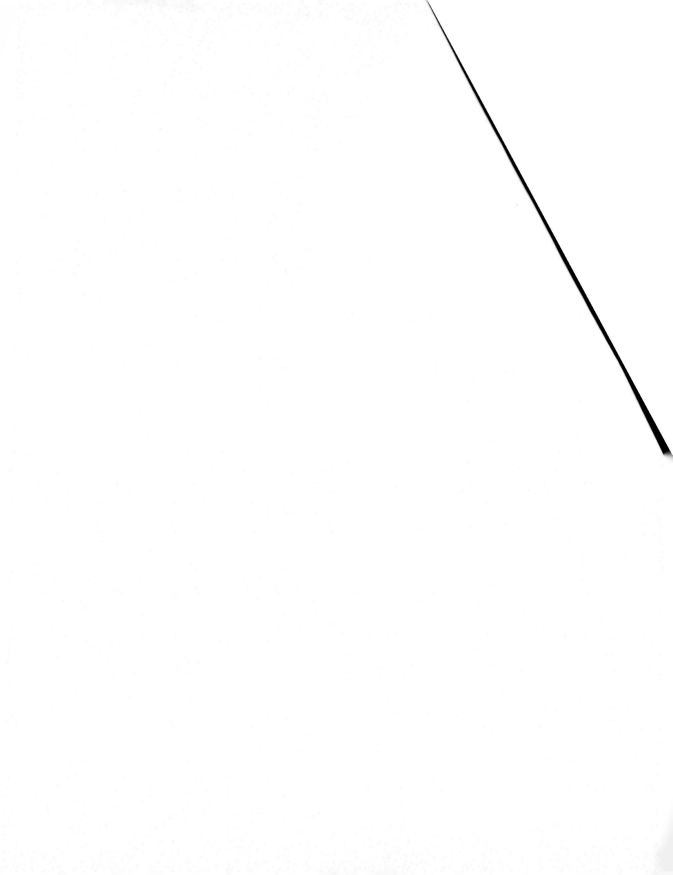